A Little Book For New Philosophers

Why And How To Study Philosophy
Paul Copan

EasyRead Large

Copyright Page from the Original Book

InterVarsity Press
P.O. Box 1400, Downers Grove, IL 60515-1426
ivpress.com
email@ivpress.com

InterVarsity Press® is the book-publishing division of InterVarsity Christian Fellowship/ USA®, a movement of students and faculty active on campus at hundreds of universities, colleges and schools of nursing in the United States of America, and a member movement of the International Fellowship of Evangelical Students. For information about local and regional activities, visit intervarsity.org.

All Scripture quotations, unless otherwise indicated, are taken from the New American Standard Bible®, copyright 1960, 1962, 1963, 1968, 1971, 1972, 1973, 1975, 1977, 1995 by The Lockman Foundation. Used by permission.

Cover design: Cindy Kiple
Interior design: Beth McGill

ISBN 978-0-8308-5147-8 (print)
ISBN 978-0-8308-9446-8 (digital)

Printed in the United States of America ∞

 *As a member of the Green Press Initiative, InterVarsity Press is committed to protecting the environment and to the responsible use of natural resources. To learn more, visit greenpressinitiative.org.*

Library of Congress Cataloging-in-Publication Data

A catalog record for this book is available from the Library of Congress.

P	18	17	16	15	14	13	12	11	10	9	8	7	6	5	4	3	2	1
Y	31	30	29	28	27	26	25	24	23	22	21	20	19	18	17	16

TABLE OF CONTENTS

"Over the last decade or so, professor Copan has risen in stature among Christians and non-Christians alike. Many look to him for counsel, for intellectual help and for spiritual wisdom. All of this and much more is incorporated into his delightful little book *A Little Book for New Philosophers.* Written with the warmth and wisdom of a pastor, yet exhibiting knowledge of an incredibly wide range of relevant philosophical literature, Copan has written the most important book to date as to what philosophy actually is (and should be) and why it is so important for all of us to study philosophy. This should be read by seminarians, people in vocational ministry and thoughtful lay folk, and is required reading as a text in worldview or apologetics classes. Today, the kingdom is moving in philosophy, and Copan's book will expand that movement considerably. What a delightful read!"

J.P. Moreland, distinguished professor of philosophy, Biola University; author of *The Soul*

"Paul Copan's book is small in size but large in importance. The audience is not just aspiring philosophers, but anyone in the church who is interested in, curious about or even suspicious of philosophy. Copan does a wonderful job of explaining what philosophy is, how it should be done and the value it has for Christians."

C. Stephen Evans, university professor of philosophy and humanities, Baylor University; professorial fellow,

Logos Institute for Analytic and Exegetical Theology, University of St. Andrews

"This little book is a rare gem! Paul Copan is the ideal guide to what makes philosophy distinctively important and crucial for the life of any intelligent Christian. If you have any suspicions or concerns about the role of the mind on the path of faith, read this book!"

Tom Morris, author of *Making Sense of It All, Philosophy for Dummies* and *The Oasis Within*

"Paul Copan's short book addresses the questions of why and how to do philosophy within the framework of a Christian worldview. It is directed primarily toward that growing host of laypersons who find themselves interested in intellectual issues and thus drawn to philosophy. It is directed secondarily toward that diminishing group of Christians who remain suspicious of the value of philosophy and still need to be convinced that this discipline can deepen their faith and equip them to serve God more effectively. The book also contains healthy reminders for philosophical veterans of the pitfalls, priorities and challenges of doing philosophical work as Christians. Paul Copan, a personal friend for many years, exemplifies the virtues that he says Christian philosophers should develop; his walk matches his talk. His reflections on this subject are convicting and humbling, making his book a worthwhile read."

William Lane Craig, research professor of philosophy, Talbot School of Theology; professor of philosophy, Houston Baptist University

"Paul Copan has a special gift for making philosophy accessible to a wide audience. Here he focuses on philosophically inclined Christians who are fearful or cynical about philosophy. He contends that philosophy done right can benefit our understanding and worship of God. I highly recommend that all Christians who doubt the value of philosophy attend to Paul Copan's lucid case. They will not be disappointed."

Paul K. Moser, professor of philosophy, Loyola University of Chicago

TO OUR DEAR SON CHRISTOPHER SOREN COPAN

A budding philosopher and a precious gift to our family. May you bear Christ's name faithfully, humbly and joyfully, with passionate inwardness and purity of heart.

PREFACE

Why a "little book" for new philosophers?

Written in the spirit of theologian Helmut Thielicke's *A Little Exercise for New Theologians,* this book looks at the *why* and the *how* of philosophy. It is first directed to philosophically inclined Christians. This includes those who are *uncertain* about philosophy: though you may appreciate the life of the mind, you may still be uninformed or unconvinced about the connection between philosophy and the Christian faith. Then there are those of you who have been at least *initiated* into philosophy: you have begun to explore it, whether formally or informally, and perhaps find it daunting or exhilarating or both. There are also the *seasoned:* you have been trained in philosophy. Perhaps you teach it or even write about it. So this book contains descriptions, suggestions, pitfalls, priorities, challenges and encouragements for Christian pilgrims in philosophy. My hope is that this small book will offer new material for some, reminders for others and, I trust, reinforcement for all to look afresh at the implications of doing philosophy under the lordship of Christ.

Second, this book is written for *philosophobic* Christians, who think philosophy is a waste of time or even deem it a spiritual compromise. Thus this book serves as a justification or defense of philosophy, which has strengthened the saints and informed the articulation of Christian doctrine across the centuries. Oxford philosopher Brian Leftow's affirmation that "it was Christianity that brought me to philosophy" is a common story across church history.[1]

Traditionally, philosophy has acted as the *ancilla theologiae*—theology's handmaid—by taking a *ministerial,* or assisting, role. Yet to assume theology's *magisterial*—that is, authoritative—role is not to denigrate philosophy but rather to praise it for performing a great service in helping us better grasp and clarify Christian doctrine. Now, Christian philosophy does not attempt to remove all mystery, nor can it fully comprehend the depths and riches of the wisdom and knowledge of God. However, by God's grace, philosophy can enhance our understanding and our worship of God, aid us in the pursuit of the life of the mind, enrich our study of the history of ideas and their justification and implications, and assist us in winsomely defending the coherence of our faith in our Lord Jesus Christ, "who became to us wisdom from God" (1 Cor 1:30).

I am grateful to IVP Academic editor Andy Le Peau for inviting me to write this book. He has been a great encouragement over the years, and I will miss his partnership as he retires from editing. IVP's Dan

---

[1] Brian Leftow, "From Jerusalem to Athens," in God and the Philosophers: The Reconciliation of Faith and Reason, ed. Thomas V. Morris (New York: Oxford University Press, 1994), 193.

Reid has stepped in to see the book through to the end, and his and Andy's insightful comments on the manuscript, along with Ethan McCarthy's, have strengthened the book. I'm thankful, too, to IVP's Jeff Crosby for his kind friendship and for his urging me to do more publishing with IVP.

I want to recognize the inspiring and encouraging philosophical mentors I have had over the years. These include my first philosophy professors—the late Stuart Hackett as well as William Lane Craig. In addition, my philosophy friends—J.P. Moreland, Gary Habermas, Francis Beckwith, Doug Geivett, David K. Clark, Ron Tacelli, Paul Moser, Charles Taliaferro and Alvin Plantinga—have been an immense help along the way, and I could add many more like Tom Morris, Nicholas Wolterstorff and Stephen Evans, who have each influenced me through their work. Thanks to my fine brother, Vic, who encouraged me to pursue an MA in philosophy in addition to an MDiv—an important step that has borne so much fruit. And I am grateful to my dear high school English teacher, Miss Nell Harden, for her loving dedication and diligence in teaching grammar, punctuation and writing. Without her influence, I would likely not be writing and editing books.

As always, I am deeply indebted to my wife, Jacqueline, a lover of wisdom and a steadfast support—a true partner with whom I share an "uncommon union."

INTRODUCTION

In recent decades God has made a comeback in philosophy departments and leading publishing houses. One atheist philosopher, Quentin Smith, has said that philosophy is becoming "denaturalized." A renaissance in Christian philosophy—along with the emergence of philosophy of religion as a discipline—has been a blessed development. However, in the mid-twentieth century this philosophical light was considerably dimmer.

In the fall of 1993, philosopher William Lane Craig and I had the privilege of meeting the iconic atheist philosopher Paul Edwards in his New York City apartment. There were a few memorable moments, like when Edwards kicked over his glass of wine on the carpet, and we observed an oddity on his apartment wall—an electric restroom hand dryer to help alleviate his neck pain. Edwards recounted how inspirational Bertrand Russell's essay "Why I Am Not a Christian" had been to him over the course of his philosophical career. This was quite a surprise to us, since Russell's arguments there are weak and sophomoric. Yet, Edwards told us, whenever he felt oppressed by some philosophical or ideological constraints, he would reread Russell's essay to help "throw off the chains" and—raising both fists in the air—"experience freedom!"

Back in 1967, the Enlightenment-style *Encyclopedia of Philosophy* first appeared in print, edited by Edwards. He acknowledged that his own atheistic "ideological commitment" gave shape to this project, which was undertaken in the spirit of such biting critics of religion as Voltaire, Diderot, Hume and Russell. In a delicious twist of irony, Christian philosopher Alvin Plantinga's sophisticated, groundbreaking book *God and Other Minds* was published that same year. Plantinga's book, atheist philosopher Quentin Smith observed, helped pave the way for the quiet revolution in Christian philosophy that followed. Another irony is this: in 1996 a supplement to Edwards's *Encyclopedia* was published to incorporate the many developments in the field since 1967. This supplement took a decidedly more theistic and religious turn, much to Edwards's dismay.[2]

There were other encyclopedic developments around the same time. In 1995 the online *Stanford Encyclopedia of Philosophy* project was launched, and in 1998 the present gold-standard—the *Routledge Encyclopedia of Philosophy,* edited by Edward Craig—was published. Both of these works are considerably more sympathetic to theism, and many

---

2 See Paul Edwards, "Introduction," in Encyclopedia of Philosophy, ed. Paul Edwards (New York: Macmillan, 1967), 1:xi; "Statement by Paul Edwards Concerning the Supplementary Volume of the Encyclopedia of Philosophy," Inquiry 41 no.1 (1998): 123-24.

of their contributors are Christians. Sophisticated books in philosophy promoting or sympathetic to theism are regularly published by mainstream presses such as Oxford, Cambridge, Wiley, Routledge and Ashgate.

Of course, we should avoid triumphalism and always put our trust in the Lord rather than in historical trends, however encouraging they may be. I offer this brief historical sketch to encourage believers interested in pursuing philosophy—as well as Christian philosophers who have been engaged in the task for years—that Christians doing good work in philosophy have earned the respect of other philosophers and a rightful place in the academy.

PART ONE

WHY STUDY PHILOSOPHY?

1

PHILOSOPHY AND BAKING BREAD

Philosophical thinking can enable us to see through objections to Christian belief; it can exhibit the faith as something plausible and intellectually respectable; it can show the faith as something that can command the assent of an educated, intellectually sophisticated and knowledgeable denizen of [the contemporary world].

WILLIAM ALSTON,
"A PHILOSOPHER'S WAY BACK TO FAITH"

***

Philosophy students share a common plight with their art and music counterparts: their parents often worry about how their children will support themselves with such an impractical degree. As you consider pursuing philosophy you will get questions like, "What kind of a job can you get with a philosophy degree?" or, "Unless you eventually become a philosophy professor, what can you *do* with philosophy?" This concern isn't a new one. The crusty old Latin dictum *philosophia panem non torrit*—"philosophy doesn't bake bread"—expresses the same sentiment, wryly but boldly.

Sustaining oneself economically is no small thing. Caring parents are right to hope that their children will eventually achieve financial independence. Yet complaints and jokes about impoverished philosophers may reveal a profoundly pragmatic, yes, *philosophy* of education: that learning is merely a means to join the workforce or to make money. But this is a narrow and shortsighted perspective that stands opposed to the more robust, classical understanding: that the good, the true and the beautiful ought to be pursued for their own sake. A proper education will take the wisdom of the past more seriously than preparing for standardized tests in the present. It will teach students *how* to think, not simply *what* to think. And it will evoke serious thought about the good life and the shaping of character. The embodiment of wisdom in human form, Jesus of Nazareth, insists that we live not only by physical bread, but by God's spirituallysustaining, satisfying words (Mt 4:4). In a very real sense, we are what we eat.

Beyond this, perhaps we could offer a few crumbs of insight for the as-yet unconvinced about philosophy's value.

Philosophy is mind-sharpening. Serious students of philosophy can attest to the value of a rigorously exercised mind. Through disciplined philosophical training, the mind—which is different from the brain—becomes both sharpened and more supple. But the brain can still get in on the action. Neuroscientists have observed that persons with, say, obsessive-compulsive disorder can choose to create new thought patterns and actions that actually result in diminishing the disorder's effects—quite evident in before and after brain scans. Likewise, pursuing intellectually stimulating disciplines like philosophy will strengthen and oil the workings of the mind, and create new neural pathways in the process. The mind is like a muscle, J.P. Moreland reminds us, and the more we exercise it, the more adept we become at using it.[3] Philosophy can facilitate clearer thinking about concepts and justification of positions.

Philosophy helps us see that ideas have consequences. The tools of philosophy—things like appropriating the laws of logic, detecting fallacies and working through arguments—can help rescue us from a multitude of intellectual sins: lazy thinking, faddishness, superficiality and blindness to powerful ideologies or other idols of modern thought and their pernicious consequences.

Human history has been shaped by many potent philosophical ideas—sometimes with devastating results, as with Marxism and social Darwinism. Historian Paul Johnson estimates that over 100 million people were

---

3   J.P. Moreland, Love Your God with All Your Mind, 2nd ed. (Colorado Springs: NavPress, 2012), 101.

killed or starved to death in the twentieth century—the tragic result of implementing philosophies that were formulated and developed in the paneled halls of the academy.[4] Studying and assessing history-shaping worldviews—whether destructive or beneficial—is no insignificant matter.

Philosophy expands our horizons. Studying philosophy enhances our thinking about a range of topics and disciplines—law, economics, politics, history, theology and science. The theoreticians and practitioners of science, for example, would do well to remember just how much their discipline depends on philosophical assumptions that they often take for granted: that the external world exists, that our sense perception is generally reliable, that the universe has a certain rational structure and follows certain patterns (scientific laws), that the universe can be studied and understood by human minds, and that inescapable logical laws enable us to theorize, make inferences and draw conclusions about the world.

Philosophy can help isolate bad or sloppy thinking. It's not just some Christians who belittle philosophy. Many in our culture's new high priesthood—the scientific community—have embraced an anti-philosophy philosophy. Physicist Stephen

---

4 Paul Johnson, Darwin: Portrait of a Genius (New York: Penguin, 2013), 136.

Hawking has proclaimed that "philosophy is dead";[5] physics must come to our rescue and provide full answers to questions about where we've come from and who we are. Similarly, biologist Richard Lewontin adopts an absolute, untestable materialism without argument—no matter how arbitrary it seems to the uninitiated.[6] This isn't science. As Del Ratzsch defines it, science is the objective study of the natural world and its phenomena; the concepts and explanations it uses don't normally depart from the natural world.[7] Rather, this is *scientism*—the arbitrary and self-contradictory belief that science alone gives us knowledge.

> The theorist who maintains that science is the be-all and end-all—that what is not in science textbooks is not worth knowing—is an ideologist with a peculiar and distorted doctrine of his own. For him, science is no longer a sector of the cognitive enterprise but

5 Stephen Hawking and Leonard Mlodinow, The Grand Design (New York: Bantam Books, 2010), 5.

6 Richard Lewontin, "Billions and Billions of Demons," New York Review of Books (January 9, 1997): 28-32.

7 Del Ratzsch, Science and Its Limits (Downers Grove, IL: InterVarsity Press, 2000), 13. Ratzsch notes that concepts about the uniformity of nature, the capacity for our minds to study the world and other theisticallygrounded assumptions about science are taken for granted—without explanation—by many nontheistic scientists.

> an all-inclusive worldview. This is the doctrine not of science but of Scientism. To take this stance is not to celebrate science but to distort it.
>
> Nicholas Rescher, *The Limits of Science*

The statements of Hawking and Lewontin are sheer bluster and confusion. For all of their "philosophobia," as Nicholas Rescher calls it, they're doing their own amateur philosophizing.[8] Taking philosophical positions is unavoidable, and the list of scientists waxing philosophical without realizing it—or worse, denying that they have a philosophy at all—is long. Rather than pitting philosophy and science against each other, we would do well to return to the old understanding of science as "natural philosophy." Rightly did C.S. Lewis prophesy about these naysayers: "Good philosophy must exist, if for no other reason, because bad philosophy needs to be answered."[9]

Philosophy can strengthen our theology. Though we will define philosophy in more detail a little later, we can say here that philosophy and theology are not, at their root, all that distinguishable. The main difference is that theology's specific focus is God—what

---

8 Nicholas Rescher, "Philosophobia," American Philosophical Quarterly 29 (July 1992): 301-2.

9 C.S. Lewis, "Learning in War-Time," in The Weight of Glory and Other Addresses (New York: Macmillan, 1965), 28.

Alister McGrath calls *discourse about God.*[10] The tools of philosophy—themselves a gift from God—can and should be applied to the knowledge of God. So we say *No!* to the false, though common, assumption that philosophy must begin *from below*—that is, with unaided human reason operating independently of God's empowering Spirit.

Since the rise of the discipline of the philosophy of religion in the second half of the twentieth century, many trained philosophers have been doing creative, cutting-edge work in the realm of Christian theology—the incarnation, the Trinity, divine foreknowledge, human freedom, providence, original sin, the inspiration of Scripture and biblical interpretation. Indeed, philosophers of religion have made a remarkable contribution to systematic theology, helping make it more robust, intellectually rigorous and conceptually precise. This specific discipline is called *analytic theology.*[11] Seminaries with good

---

10 Alister E. McGrath, Christian Theology: An Introduction (Oxford: Wiley-Blackwell, 2011), 102. David K. Clark rightly claims that the task of theology is to "articulate the content of the gospel of Jesus Christ to the context of a particular culture." To Know and Love God: Method for Theology (Wheaton, IL: Crossway, 2002), 33. In his volume, Clark—a trained philosopher—presents much wise guidance concerning the task of theology.

11 For a splendid overview of this discipline, as well as a sound response to the misconceptions surrounding it, see

philosophy programs will undoubtedly help sharpen their theology, biblical studies and counseling/psychology departments. This crossfertilization of ideas will contribute to a better integrated, wellrounded learning environment. Although it's Christ, not philosophy, who holds all things together, a Christ-centered philosophy program is a great good that will prove to be a resourceful handmaiden at any theological institution.

> I found this philosophy alone to be safe and profitable. Thus, and for this reason, I am a philosopher.
>
> Justin Martyr, *Second Apology*

This applies to the academy in general. Unfortunately, from the 1870s onward the academy has become more and more of a disintegrated multiversity than a university. The United States has witnessed a general fragmentation of the academic disciplines in higher education.[12] The "specialization" phenomenon has contributed to expertise, on the one hand. Yet it has also created a compartmentalization and ignorance of the broader world, fittingly illustrated by the naïve

---

Thomas H. McCall, An Invitation to Analytic Christian Theology (Downers Grove, IL: IVP Academic, 2015).

[12] Jon H. Roberts and James Turner, The Sacred and the Secular University (Princeton, NJ: Princeton University Press, 2000).

comments of scientists like Hawking and Lewontin. Such academic tunnel vision is the result of abandoning our Christian moorings and the biblical vision of the world as God's creation. With the Lord's help, the growth of Christian philosophy and the presence of respected Christian philosophers in influential universities can offer a strong integrative response to this academic fragmentation and can demonstrate the unifying and explanatory power of the Christian faith.

Some readers may have a deeper concern, though. The conventional view in many churches is that, more often than not, the study of philosophy erodes faith and creates barriers to belief. Many Christian pastors have cautioned the youth in their congregations: "Don't study philosophy in university. It will ruin your faith!" These well-meaning guides may even think their admonitions are biblically justified. They may string together a biblical-sounding mantra: "The gospel is foolishness to those who are perishing. The natural person doesn't understand spiritual matters. We should beware of philosophy. Those who believe without having seen are more blessed than those who believe because they have seen."

So perhaps we should be clear about what philosophy is, and then explore whether Scripture actually directs us away from it—or toward it.

2

PHILOSOPHY AS LOVING WISDOM

And should we not desire to have our minds in the best state possible?

SOCRATES IN PLATO'S
HIPPIAS MINOR

PHILOSOPHY AT ITS ROOT

What is philosophy? Etymologies—the origins or roots of words—don't necessarily reveal a word's actual meaning. For instance, our word *nice* comes from the Latin *nescius*—"ignorant." We do considerably better with the etymology of the word *philosophy;* it comes from the Greek words *philia* ("love") and *sophia* ("wisdom"). Thus philosophy is "the love of wisdom." According to Socrates, wisdom entails humility. For Aristotle, we cannot be wise without being good.[13] These ancient philosophers saw their philosophical endeavors as bound up with wisdom.

---

[13] See Plato, Apology 20e-23c; Aristotle, Nichomachean Ethics VI.

The metaphysician Richard Taylor once recalled being with some academic philosophers. A college dean who was present asked them to answer the question, "What is philosophy?" After a long, awkward silence, Taylor suggested that philosophy begins with the basic "love of wisdom." His answer drew giggles and laughter from the other philosophers—it was something so basic yet so removed from their philosophizing.[14] As Jesus rebuked the religious leaders of his time for straining out gnats but swallowing camels—that is, being obsessed with the minutiae of the law but overlooking the fundamentals of justice, mercy and faithfulness—Taylor's words served as a similar rebuke of these philosophers for overlooking the fundamental love at the heart of their craft.

Despite the loftiness often associated with philosophy, the reputation of philosophers has been a mixed bag. Satirist H.L. Mencken defined philosophy this way: "Philosophy consists largely of one philosopher arguing that all the others are jackasses. He usually proves it, and I should add that he usually proves that he is one himself."[15] The Enlightenment critic Voltaire purportedly had a similar opinion: "When he who hears doesn't know what he who speaks means, and when

---

14 Tim Madigan, "Interview: Richard Taylor," Philosophy Now 40 (March/April 2003).

15 H.L. Mencken, Minority Report (New York: Knopf, 1956), 55.

he who speaks doesn't know what he himself means—that is philosophy."[16] Michel de Montaigne confessed about his own discipline: "Wonder is the foundation of all philosophy, inquiry the process, ignorance the end."[17] And the Roman philosopher Cicero observed, "Somehow or other no statement is too absurd for some philosophers to make."[18] If this is the sum of philosophy, it's not a very encouraging start for aspiring students. What's more, it reflects poorly on those within the guild itself—although these philosophers can at least agree on one thing: philosophers disagree on virtually any topic they study!

IS PHILOSOPHY A NEUTRAL OR SECULAR WORLDVIEW?

Many—including Christians—assume that philosophy is a worldview in itself: a particular system of belief or a fully orbed way of life. They assume that philosophy

---

16 Taken from Tom Morris, Philosophy for Dummies (New York: IDG Books, 1999), 14.

17 Michel de Montaigne, Complete Essays, trans. Donald M. Frame (Stanford, CA: Stanford University Press, 1958), 788.

18 Cicero, On Divination 2.58, in On Old Age; On Friendship; On Divination, trans. W.A. Falconer, Loeb Classical Library 154 (Cambridge, MA: Harvard University Press, 1923), 507.

is atheistic or secular by definition. Agnostic philosopher Luc Ferry takes this view: "The quest for salvation without God is at the heart of every great philosophical system.... Philosophy also claims to save us—if not from death itself, then from the anxiety it causes, and to do so by the exercise of our own resources in our innate faculty of reason."[19] Philosophy, he claims, is the endeavor to find salvation without God, to reason without blind faith, to pursue freedom instead of faith—all in the quest to overcome the fear of death. Ferry is onto something in connecting philosophy and death. Plato and the Roman philosopher Cicero both affirmed that philosophy's purpose is to prepare us for death. However, Ferry is wrong to assume that philosophy's default position is secularism. The theologian would call this selfsought salvation *Pelagianism;* it is a manifestation of the worst of the seven deadly sins—pride. If God is brought into philosophical discussion, why does it suddenly cease to be philosophy and become religion? This is arbitrary and false.

> Those who really apply themselves in the right way to philosophy are directly and of their own accord preparing themselves for dying and death.
>
> Plato, *The Phaedo*

---

19 Luc Ferry, A Brief History of Thought: A Philosophical Guide to Living (New York: Harper Perennial, 2011), 72-73.

Historically speaking, Ferry's is an inaccurate, selective view of philosophy. First, if it's true that Pythagoras (c. 570–495BC) came up with the term *philosophy,* we should remember that he considered wisdom to be something divine. What's more, he believed that mortals could aspire to this divinity as "lovers" of wisdom.

Second, a casual survey of the history of philosophy reveals a host of Christian titans. Consider Augustine, Anselm, Albert the Great, Aquinas, Alston and Adams—and those are just some of the A's!

Third, ironically, the term *religion* itself is impossibly vague and difficult to define. There are at least seventeen definitions according to religion scholar Martin Marty.[20] Like it or not, philosophy and God or "the divine" have had a long history together.

Fourth, as we'll soon see, the Christian faith—what Ferry calls "religion"—was considered a philosophy in the first-century Mediterranean world. Philosophy and traditional religion have overlapped throughout history. Usually people associate religion with a focus on the sacred or transcendent and how they furnish purpose and meaning for our lives; but "philosophy" has often stepped across these kinds of lines. Consider Plato's

---

[20] Martin E. Marty with Jonathan Moore, Politics, Religion, and the Common Good (San Francisco: Jossey-Bass, 2000), 10.

focus on the "transcendentals" and otherworldly "forms" around which we should order our lives.

I recall my first philosophy professor, Stuart Hackett, saying, "Everyone is a philosopher." Everyone takes a philosophical view of things—a worldview, some call it—even if their philosophical assumptions are subconscious and unexplored. Like it or not, whatever your outlook or training, you are a philosopher!

Bertrand Russell said that behind every philosophy is a "concealed metaphysic."[21] We all have a view of what is ultimately *real* (metaphysics): Is matter the only reality that exists? Is the external world an illusion? Does a Creator God exist? Do we have free will? Is there life after death? In addition, we all have views about *knowledge* (epistemology): What is knowledge? Can we truly know? If so, how do we come to know things? Finally, we all take a stance on *value* and *virtue* (axiology): What is the good life? What is right and wrong? Is beauty simply in the eye of the beholder? You see, we all take a stance and assume some answers to these questions, whether consciously or not.

Furthermore, the philosophical underpinnings by which we operate—whether explored or unexplored—reflect our deeper heart commitments. As the philosopher

---

21 Bertrand Russell, The Basic Writings of Bertrand Russell, 1903–1959, ed. Robert E. Egher and Lester E. Denonn (New York: Simon & Schuster, 1963), 191.

J.G. Fichte noted, our philosophies (or worldviews) are not merely intellectual and detached—what he called "a dead piece of furniture."[22] Rather, they are animated by our soul. They are deeply personal, bound up with who we are at our core.

Thus it is no surprise that philosophers across history are preoccupied with two interrelated concerns: rigorous thought and virtuous living. Deep contemplation about the true, the good and the beautiful cannot be separated from living it out.

Every person has a philosophy of life. The discipline of philosophy involves examining a vast array of philosophies across history—not just secular ones that seek a this-worldly salvation. Philosophy is not one particular philosophy of life. We shouldn't think, *This is what Philosophy says.* And our philosophy of life—whether we are theists, atheists or Hindus—will inevitably lead us to make truth-claims, which stand in need of justification as we engage with others. The atheist or secularist can't hide behind the Oz-like curtain of "what Philosophy says"—as though this is a cover for some allegedly detached, objective, default view by which all others are to be judged. When we pull this curtain away, there stands a person with *a* philosophy—just like all the rest of us. And that

---

22 J.G. Fichte, The Science of Knowledge, ed. and trans. Peter Heath and John Lachs (Cambridge: Cambridge University Press, 1982), 16.

person's philosophy of life can't simply be asserted. It must be justified.

PHILOSOPHY AS A TOOL

Another way of looking at philosophy is as a kind of tool. In this sense it is a *way* of thinking, not the *result* of your thinking. Socrates took this approach. He described himself as both a gadfly and a midwife. As a gadfly, he sought to rouse that "large and well-bred horse" grown sluggish—namely, the city-state of Athens. He tried to make it a better place by asking provocative questions and issuing stinging rebukes. As a midwife, he believed his task was to help others give birth to thoughtfully crafted ideas. Indeed, Socrates, who often serves as Plato's mouthpiece, would ask about how to define virtue, justice, knowledge or time. After all, as he insisted in the *Meno* dialogue, we don't have knowledge of a thing unless we can define it. While this is not absolutely so—indeed, philosophers have wrestled mightily with how precisely to define knowledge itself!—there is something to this. Philosophy itself presents us with various tools of logic and analysis for doing so.

> The usefulness of historical knowledge in philosophy ... is that the prejudices of our own period may lose their grip on us if we imaginatively enter into another period, when people's prejudices were different.

Peter Geach, *Mental Acts*

Let's extend this idea a bit. Consider how a historian might study the events that gave rise to the Reformation or the Enlightenment. This kind of study is called a "first-order" discipline. But philosophy can assist the historian, serving as a tool to analyze, clarify and systematize the concepts, questions, practices and assumptions used in the historian's work. This is the "second-order" discipline of the philosophy of history.

Philosopher Thomas Nagel shows how philosophy can serve as a tool for a variety of disciplines and facets of life:

> The main concern of philosophy is to question and understand very common ideas that all of us use every day without thinking about them. The historian asks about what happened in time past, but the philosopher will ask about whether history itself has meaning or what time is. Math teachers instruct their students about numbers, but the philosopher asks, "What is a number? Are numbers real?" A physicist will study atoms and their activity whereas the philosopher will ask whether a mind-independent reality exists and what is the nature of causality. A moviegoer might wonder about whether slipping into a theater without paying is morally permissible, but the philosopher

will ask, "What makes an act right or wrong? What is the basis of morality?"

We couldn't get along in life without taking the ideas of time, number, knowledge, language, right and wrong for granted most of the time; but in philosophy we investigate those things themselves.[23]

The value of philosophy has become so pronounced and so widespread that we can find a "philosophy of" virtually any discipline or practice—psychology, sociology, history, education. Tom Morris's *If Aristotle Ran General Motors* probes questions about the good life, virtue, beauty and the nature of work as they relate to business. And book upon book is being written about the philosophy of films like *The Matrix,* TV shows like *The Simpsons* and even the place of superheroes in our cultural understanding. And though the physicist Stephen Hawking may make dismissive philosophical comments about philosophy, we can affirm a proper place for the philosophy of science.

It is probably true that we ourselves do not really understand what we are doing until we can explain it from the beginning to someone who not only does

---

23 Thomas Nagel, What Does It All Mean? A Very Short Introduction to Philosophy (New York: Oxford University Press, 1987), 5.

> not know any of the background literature but also does not know why anybody would care about such matters.
>
> Linda Zagzebski, "Vocatio Philosophiae," in *Philosophers Who Believe*

Socrates said that the unexamined life is not worth living. Now, reflection doesn't guarantee the result of a life worth living. Kai Nielsen concluded that reason can't bring us to morality, and then said, "The picture I have painted for you is not a pleasant one. Reflection on it depresses me."[24] For some worldviews, an examined life can be depressing. By contrast, Socrates believed in a kind of design-plan—that we flourish when we live according to a certain transcendent pattern. And the Christian would affirm that the more an examined life is rooted in our design and finds meaning in it, the greater depth it will have.

Someone may object: "Doesn't this life-worth-living scenario arbitrarily presume design or purpose? Doesn't this simply beg the question?" Later, we will offer reasons for taking God and design seriously, but we can say here that (1) to simply reject design is also to take a non-neutral philosophical stance, which calls for justification; (2) the critic's question is itself

---

[24] Kai Nielsen, "Why Should I Be Moral? Revisited," American Philosophical Quarterly 21 (January 1984): 90.

purposeful, directed toward receiving a coherent and intelligible answer; (3) properly-functioning rational powers assume a certain purposeful appropriation of logical laws that are presumably directed toward the truth; and (4) we humans seem inescapably preoccupied with "why" questions—a feature basic to our existence—which may be a further indicator of a goal-directed reality. It appears we cannot escape design or purpose!

From the vantage point of learning about our world, we can gain much insight from applying this "examined life" principle to all manner of disciplines and areas of study and exploration. Without these tools of philosophy to help strengthen our grasp of them and make them more vibrant, our understanding of the world would be fairly flat and insipid.

PHILOSOPHY AS HARD THINKING

Defining philosophy is a bit elusive. Yes, it involves loving wisdom, but what is the key or essential feature that ties together all philosophy? Christian philosopher Dallas Willard has described it as "an attempt to figure out the best way to live, what the best ways *to be* and *to do* are."[25] This seems to focus things a bit too narrowly, though. Alvin Plantinga has said that

---

[25] Dallas Willard, The Allure of Gentleness: Defending the Faith in the Manner of Jesus (New York: HarperOne, 2015), 41.

philosophical reflection is "not much different from just thinking hard."[26] Others have summed it up as "thinking about thinking." As we've noted, philosophy has focused on the "big questions" of *metaphysics* (the study of ultimate reality), *epistemology* (the study of knowledge and the justification of belief) and *axiology/ethics* (value, beauty, right and wrong, duty, virtue). Philosophy attempts to clarify concepts, formulate arguments, justify positions and integrate ideas into a coherent worldview.

Philosophers, however, have begun from vastly differing starting points and assumptions about sources of knowledge. Consider these extremes. There's Plato, who diminished the physical world and located knowledge in the eternal, unchanging realm of the forms of truth, goodness and beauty. By contrast, David Hume and the logical positivists who followed him anchored knowledge in sense experience. So how we do philosophy may be shaped by the era or community in which we find ourselves.

What of *theology*—the study of God? This too involves philosophizing. That is, we are to think hard about God's self-revelation in creation, conscience, reason and human experience (*general* revelation) as well as in Jesus of Nazareth and in Scripture (*special* revelation). In fact, we could rightly call Jesus a

---

26 Alvin Plantinga, God, Freedom, and Evil (Grand Rapids: Eerdmans, 1977), 1.

philosopher, since he embodied divine wisdom and spoke with intelligence and profundity about being, knowledge and value.

Philosophical reflection can enhance our grasp of the Christian faith. Princeton's Diogenes Allen regularly taught his theology students about the place of philosophy in their discipline: "Everyone needs to know some philosophy in order to understand the major doctrines of Christianity or to read a great theologian intelligently.... Philosophical knowledge enables one to appreciate more deeply the meaning of virtually every major doctrinal formulation and every major theologian."[27] For example, to think coherently about the doctrine of the Trinity we must know the meaning of philosophical terms such as "substance," "being," "essence." To properly grasp Augustine's *Confessions* we must have some understanding of Neoplatonism. The same goes for knowing Aristotle in order to understand Aquinas.

The early church fathers engaged the philosophical world of their day to show that the Christian faith had solid intellectual merits to challenge the ideologies and heresies of their era. While some outsiders did come into the church through such intellectual defenses (Augustine, for example), the greater effect

---

[27] Diogenes Allen, Philosophy for Understanding Theology (Atlanta: John Knox Press, 1985), iii-iv.

was the confidence their intellectual labors gave to believers that their faith was rational and defensible.

We observed earlier that, in recent years, formally-trained Christian philosophers have done a good deal of significant, sophisticated work in the discipline of analytic theology—(also called "the philosophy of theology" or "analytic philosophical theology"). These thinkers have helped clarify doctrinal categories and offered rigorous argumentation—not unlike the work of Augustine, Anselm, Aquinas and John Calvin. Moreover, contrary to certain theologians' accusations, many have done so with a close eye on the history of theology and with a view toward the spiritual formation of their readers. These analytic theologians haven't focused primarily on Christian apologetics or arguments for God's existence, nor have they locked themselves into abstract philosophical categories devoid of warmhearted devotion to Christ.

The thought of Jonathan Edwards (1703–1758), the eighteenth-century theologian, pastor and missionary, has received much worthy attention in recent scholarship, and a large part of his work is deep philosophy. One of the most brilliant minds America has ever produced, he studied Scripture as well as the latest philosophical and scientific ideas. Influenced by Platonism, he drew from philosophers such as Nicolas Malebranche, the Cambridge Platonists and John Locke, and he took their lines of thought in creative theological directions. He would apply his rigorous logical mind to the reshaping and unifying of these ideas in the pursuit of the triune God's glory. Edwards appropriated the tools of philosophy in a distinctively Christian manner, and those who study his work have profited greatly from his philosophical precision and theological creativity.

> [Jonathan Edwards's] intellectual project could be characterized as an attempt to re-envision Reformed theology using aspects of early Enlightenment philosophy. Rather than regarding with suspicion all the literary products of the 'new philosophy' ... Edwards thought of these authors as providing (among other things) new tools by means of which he could undergird Christian theology.
>
> Oliver Crisp, *Jonathan Edwards among the Theologians*

Edwards's theological counterpart in England, Oxford-trained John Wesley (1703–1791), took much the same view on the importance of the life of the mind and the place of philosophy. In his "Address to the Clergy" (1756) he urged pastors to be familiar not only with biblical languages and the fine points of theology, but also with history, natural philosophy (science), metaphysics and logic. He even said that knowledge of geometry is important: it is not only useful in itself, but it also helps "give clearness of apprehension, and an habit of thinking closely and connectedly."[28]

The philosophically informed, thoughtful sermons and writings of both Edwards and Wesley serve as a model for pastors and other Christian leaders today. Their clarity and insight were certainly not in conflict with their dependence on the Spirit's power.

---

[28] John Wesley, The Works of the Reverent John Wesley, vol.6 (New York: J. Emory and B. Waugh, 1831), 219.

3

FAITH, PHILOSOPHY AND SCRIPTURE

It is hard to think of a topic in systematic theology where analytic philosophical work cannot be illuminating.

WILLIAM ABRAHAM, "TURNING PHILOSOPHICAL WATER INTO THEOLOGICAL WINE"

FAITH: ITS CHARACTER AND ITS CARICATURES

Faith is a much-abused term these days. Some claim that faith is mere opinion or unsupported belief. Unlike science, they argue, faith ignores reasons, denies evidence and doesn't get results. Mark Twain defined faith as "believing what you know ain't so"; others have claimed it's pretending to know what you don't know. Actually, it's these critics who pretend to know what they don't know about faith. Of course, a number of traditional religions and even the average Christian may be indifferent to reasons for belief. Indeed, surveys of professing Christians often reveal that they are Christians just because it's the belief they grew up with, and not because they understand the Christian faith to be true independent of their upbringing. They tend to assume that good reasons and faith are contradictory notions. Yet no Christian theologian would view faith this way. Such pseudo-definitions run counter to the robust intellectual tradition of the historic Christian faith.

Genuine faith is truth-directed, not truth-denying. It invites intellectual inquiry and appeals to evidence such as signs and wonders or eyewitness testimony. Consider Augustine's dictum, "I believe that I may understand" *(credo ut intelligam)* and Anselm's, "Faith seeking understanding" *(fides quaerens intellectum).* Both assume that trust in God ("I believe") is the first step in the journey to better comprehend how we ought to think and live before God in this world ("...that I may understand"). These thinkers repudiated evidence-resistance or truthavoidance since true biblical faith is not opposed to reason. Rather, they rightly understood faith to be a *volitional* stance of trust in God, and this choice enabled them to see reality more clearly. C.S. Lewis expressed their stance this way: "I believe in Christianity as I believe that the sun has risen, not only because I see it, but because by it I see everything else."[29]

---

[29] C.S. Lewis, "Is Theology Poetry?" in The Weight of Glory and Other Addresses (New York: Macmillan, 1965), 140.

Although he grew up in an anti-intellectual North African Christendom, Augustine came to appreciate the philosophical strength of the Christian faith through Ambrose of Milan. As though speaking in our own day, Augustine wrote in his *Literal Meaning of Genesis* about how disgraceful it is for ill-informed Christians to talk science with well-informed, scientifically-minded unbelievers. If Christians speak such falsehoods about science and other areas of study, will these unbelievers—who know the "facts which they themselves have learnt from experience and the light of reason"[30]—take Christians seriously on topics like the resurrection of the dead, the hope of eternal life, or God's kingdom?

FAITH AND KNOWLEDGE

In our culture, many—alas, even some Christians!—pit faith against knowledge. It is assumed that faith is simply opinion, closed off from scrutiny, something restricted to the private life. While this may be true in other traditional religions, this is a far cry from the biblical faith, which is a *knowledge tradition* (Jn 17:3; 2 Pet 1:5-8; 1 Jn 1:1-5). To have genuine faith is to have genuine knowledge: Scripture connects the two, rather than dividing or compartmentalizing them. Indeed, what good is a faith disconnected from

---

30 Augustine, The Literal Meaning of Genesis 1.19, Ancient Christian Writers 41, trans. John Hammond Taylor, S.J. (New York: Paulist Press,1982), 43.

knowledge and not rooted in reality? Faith without knowledge is dead. It is incapable of properly guiding our actions or our worship. True faith—and thus knowledge—can and should inform how we engage in the public square, and it brings illumination and insight to a wide range of intellectual disciplines. A privatized faith is not a biblical one: "We cannot stop speaking about what we have seen and heard" (Acts 4:20).

Scripture is replete with knowledge claims, evidence and credible witnesses. Luke "investigated everything carefully" so that Theophilus "may know the exact truth" about Jesus' significance (Lk 1:3-4). The beloved disciple was "testifying" concerning Jesus' life, death and resurrection, "and we know that his testimony is true" (Jn 21:24). Jesus demonstrated his resurrection "by many convincing proofs ... over a period of forty days" (Acts 1:3). As a designated apostle to the Gentiles, Paul emphasizes, "I am telling the truth, I am not lying" (1 Tim 2:7; cf. Rom 9:1; 2 Cor 11:31; Gal 1:20). John tells his readers that he is writing to them "so that you may know that you have eternal life" (1 Jn 5:13).

Still, some people claim the Bible teaches that faith is opposed to reason. Why engage in philosophy when the gospel is "foolishness to those who are perishing" (1 Cor 1:18)? If the "natural" person considers spiritual things "foolishness" (1 Cor 2:14), why offer arguments? Doesn't Paul warn us against "philosophy and empty deception" (Col 2:8)? Jesus himself tells Thomas the Doubter that those who *haven't* seen the resurrected Jesus and still believe are "blessed" (Jn 20:29). Maybe philosophy is more than a waste of time; maybe it is a spiritual danger.

As we'll see, such antiphilosophy claims are a mishandling of biblical texts. In fact, they are antispiritual and antitheological: they insult the Spirit of truth (Jn 16:13) and the God who calls on his image-bearers to "reason together" (Is 1:18). The biblical faith is founded on evidences that are often publicly available and on powerful displays of signs and wonders. The word *faith* is primarily personal; it refers to our trust in and commitment to Christ. But this trusting commitment is no blind leap. It is wellgrounded. Think of the act of choosing a spouse: we should have good reasons to commit to someone in marriage, but even so the marriage can't happen without a personal choice.

Biblical faith is far removed from common cultural definitions and from the faith of many other traditional religions. It is a knowledge tradition. While it is personal, it is not private.

ALL TRUTH IS GOD'S TRUTH

To possess biblical faith is to be concerned about—not fearful of—the truth. Paul insists on this: if Christ were not raised from the dead, the Christian faith would be false and should not be believed; just eat, drink and be merry, for tomorrow we die (1 Cor 15:13-14, 32). As theologian Jaroslav Pelikan put it, "If Christ is risen, then nothing else matters. And if Christ is not risen, then nothing else matters."[31]

Some Christians insist that they "believe only the Bible." Actually, they don't. They probably won't consult the Bible when it comes to facts about chemistry, physics or geology. But whatever the source, we should be seekers of truth. To seek truth may take us *beyond* the Bible, but never *against* it. Because Christ rules over every square inch of the universe and, indeed, over all reality, all truth is his. Now, true apostles have sometimes spoken or acted falsely—think of Peter's moral and theological compromise when he separated himself from Gentile believers in Antioch (Gal 2:11-17). And even false prophets may say something true. The Scottish writer George MacDonald wrote that truth is truth—whether from the lips of Jesus or of the pagan prophet Balaam (Num 24:15-24).[32]

> All the wisdom of the world belongs to Jesus the Messiah in the first place, so any flickers or glimmers of light, anywhere in the world, are to be used and indeed celebrated within the exposition of the gospel.
>
> N.T. Wright, *Paul and the Faithfulness of God*

---

[31] Quoted in Martin E. Marty, "Professor Pelikan," The Christian Century, June 13, 2006, 47.

[32] C.S. Lewis, ed., George MacDonald: An Anthology (New York: Macmillan, 1978), 7.

In a March 1647 sermon before the House of Commons at Westminster, Cambridge philosopher Ralph Cudworth said this:

> All true knowledge does of itself naturally tend to God, who is the fountain of it, and would ever be raising our souls up upon its wings there, did we not detain it and hold it down in unrighteousness.... All philosophy to a wise man, to a truly sanctified mind ... is but matter for Divinity to work on. Religion is the queen of all those inward endowments of the soul, and all pure natural knowledge, all virgin and undeflowered arts and sciences are her handmaids, that rise up and call her blessed.[33]

All creation belongs to the Lord, and so all true academic disciplines are worthy of study. We must think Christianly about them. We should welcome God's general self-revelation in nature, conscience, reason and human experience (Ps 19:1-2; Rom 1:19-21)—and, of course, his special revelation in Christ and in Scripture. We can read God's "two books"—his works and his Word. Clearly understood, these will embrace and reinforce, rather than contradict, each other.

---

[33] In Charles Taliaferro and Alison J. Teply, eds., Cambridge Platonist Spirituality (Mahwah, NJ: Paulist Press, 2004), 57.

The imagery of farming in Isaiah 28:23-29 illustrates the point. Here God is indirectly teaching the lessons of nature to the farmer. The farmer isn't necessarily a believer in God, but God is instructing him. The farmer makes observations about the soil, seeds, fertilizer, tilling, sowing and harvesting. But who gives insight about when and how to plow the soil, how to plant various types of seed and how to harvest them? God does! "For his God instructs and teaches him properly.... This also comes from the Lord of hosts, who has made His counsel wonderful and His wisdom great" (Is 28:26, 29). The same could be said about philosophers, who reflect, study and discern truths about the world. It is God who sheds light and gives them insight about metaphysical, epistemological and ethical realities. He makes all of these available for our study and our delight (Ps 111:2).

> When the one God of gods is thought of, even by those who recognize, invoke, and worship other gods either in Heaven or on earth, He is thought of in such a way that the thought seeks to attain something than which there is nothing better or more sublime.
>
> Augustine, *On Christian Doctrine*

No wonder Paul quotes pagan philosophers and poets like Epimenides, Aratus and Menander (Acts 17:28; 1 Cor 15:33). Why should we be surprised when Paul and other biblical writers include character qualities from pagan virtue lists—self-control, courage, endurance—and Christianize them? After all, Jesus is God's agent in the world (Acts 17:31). Not only does he fulfill the Old Testament, but he is the historical embodiment of the best of the world's philosophies, ethical ideals and epic stories. He satisfies our deepest human longings and aspirations. Because Jesus is the archetypal human being—the image of God and the second Adam—all that is wise and noble and good and excellent points to him.

J.R.R. Tolkien, author of *The Lord of the Rings* and a master mythmaker himself, observed that the message of the gospel contains "all the essence of fairy-stories." Fairy tale and history come together in the person of Jesus of Nazareth. The fairy story of the gospel, Tolkien maintains, has the "inner consistency of reality." This story, which begins and ends with joy of the most exalted kind, is historically embodied without losing its deeper cosmic significance. The gospel "has not abrogated legends; it has hallowed them, especially the 'happy ending.'"[34] As C.S. Lewis observed, in Jesus—the Word who became flesh and dwelt among us (Jn 1:14)—"myth became fact."[35]

---

34 J.R.R. Tolkien, "On Fairy Stories," in Essays Presented to Charles Williams, ed. C.S. Lewis (Oxford: Oxford University Press, 1947), 38-89.

35 C.S. Lewis, "Myth Became Fact," in God in the Dock (Grand Rapids: Eerdmans, 1970), 54-60.

ANTIPHILOSOPHY BIBLICAL TEXTS?

So what about those alleged antiphilosophy texts in Scripture? Actually, we can quickly dispatch these trumped-up charges. In the case of 1 Corinthians 1–2, which talk about the folly of the cross and human inability to grasp the things of the Spirit, Paul is opposing pride, not reason. Reason is itself a gift from God. Yet we must humble ourselves to follow the Crucified One; his death of nakedness, shame and public humiliation was a curse to Jews and idiocy to Gentiles. The cross calls us—philosophers included—to abandon our self-sufficiency, pride and idolatries and to humbly repent.

Beyond this, Christian critics of philosophy and rigorous reasoning should read 1 Corinthians in its entirety. Many stop after chapter two, about the natural person who lacks spiritual insight. But keep reading. First Corinthians 15 presents a reasoned historical argument for Jesus' bodily resurrection, including a list of witnesses to this event. And then we have Colossians 2:8, which warns: "See to it that no one takes you captive through hollow and deceptive philosophy" (NIV). The apostle Paul doesn't oppose Christ-centered philosophy, but an all-toohuman philosophy that relies, as Paul says, on human tradition and "the elemental spiritual forces of this world" rather than on Christ (Col 2:20 NIV). In this particular context, Paul has in mind an early version of Gnosticism—an antiphysical philosophy that promoted an elitist, inner-circle access to secret knowledge. This particular elitist philosophy produced arrogance. Paul would say that there's proud philosophy, and there's humble philosophy. There's good philosophy, and there's bad philosophy—and the bad philosophy needs to be answered.

What of Jesus' rebuke to Thomas in John 20? He blesses those who do not see, but still believe. Again, the antiphilosophy Christian should keep reading. What immediately follows is mention of faith-conducive signs: "Therefore many other signs Jesus also performed in the presence of the disciples, which are not written in this book; but these have been written so that you may believe that Jesus is the Christ, the Son of God; and that believing you may have life in His name" (Jn 20:30-31).

Four things are noteworthy here. First, instead of refusing to believe till he had seen Jesus and touched Jesus' wounds, Thomas should have listened and been "blessed" by heeding his closest friends' reliable testimony, "We have seen the Lord!" (verse 25). Second, the author concludes by emphasizing that the evidential weight of Jesus' miracles warrants belief in him. Third, by way of reinforcement, John later speaks of having heard, seen and "touched [Jesus] with our hands" (1 Jn 1:1). Fourth, the abundance of biblical signs and wonders throughout Scripture—evidences that call for trust in the Lord—are particularly noteworthy in John's Gospel and in Acts, where we see the language of "eyewitnesses," "signs," "persuasion," "reason," "defense" and so on.

> I am a philosopher because I am a Christian.
>
> Brian Leftow, *Philosophical Scriptures*

Some Christians might argue that defending the Christian faith is to engage in apologetic violence, to be power-crazed or to label people as unbelievers. This is simply a bad apologetic against using Christian apologetics. Such arguments tend to ignore the Scriptures, which actually appeal to objective reasons quite routinely. And despite the "us versus them" charge, there's plenty of biblical language that uses believer-unbeliever categories. Jesus speaks of those belonging to "the world," and the apostles do the same. "We are from God.... He who is not from God does not listen to us" (1 Jn 4:6). Evidence and argument in no way undermine the need for divine grace; indeed, God's Spirit can use such evidences and signs to awaken faith in us. In fact, many Christians have come to faith—or have had their faith strengthened—through good reasons and evidences, through signs and wonders.

PHILOSOPHICAL SCRIPTURES

Those who doubt the place of philosophy in the Christian faith should look no further than the Old Testament book of Ecclesiastes. It explores issues of fatalism, hedonism, nihilism, human nature, mortality, meaning and purpose—common topics in philosophy class. Ecclesiastes speaks with two voices, which reflect two different philosophies of life. The first is the cynical, fatalistic and provocative Preacher who serves as Solomon's foil and explores life's deepest questions (Eccles 12:9-11). He thinks of God as distant and unconcerned, wisdom as overrated, death as the great leveler that undercuts moral endeavor and virtue, and temporal pleasure as ultimately meaningless. The Teacher often sounds strikingly similar to Bertrand Russell in his essay "A Free Man's Worship": all human labor, love, genius, achievement and heroism are destined to extinction with the solar system's death, and any philosophical perspective that has any hope of rational respectability must be built on the "firm foundation of unyielding despair."[36]

The second voice gives the godly perspective. It urges us to fear God and keep the commandments of the one who calls us all to account (Eccles 12:12-14). Rather than warning us away from philosophy, Ecclesiastes uses philosophical topics to point us to a personal, concerned, righteous God who gives life purpose and will bring cosmic justice in the end.[37]

---

[36] Bertrand Russell, "A Free Man's Worship," in Mysticism and Logic and Other Essays (London: Allen & Unwin, 1963), 41.

[37] See Tremper Longman, The Book of Ecclesiastes, NICOT (Grand Rapids: Eerdmans, 1998).

The book of Job assumes the reality of evil and innocent suffering, and is often cited in discussions and books of philosophy. It presents a personal, wise Creator at the heart of reality. This Creator shows tender care for all the things he has made, including Job. The book uses maternal and paternal images to show this care (38:8-9, 28-29), and throughout the book God reveals meticulous concern and provision for his creation—animate and inanimate. When Job receives that longed-for face-to-face encounter with God, all of his objections and anger melt away.

Perhaps a surprising place to find a robust affirmation of philosophy is in the life and writings of the convert Paul of Tarsus—which was "no insignificant city" (Acts 21:39). Tarsus was the very birthplace and center of Stoic philosophy. Is Paul among the philosophers? Yes! Luke intentionally presents him as a Christian Socrates in Athens, using the language of Plato's *Apology* to describe his teacher's activities. Both Socrates and Paul reasoned with others in the marketplace; they both brought a "new" teaching; and they were both described as promoting strange or foreign deities. Paul quoted Stoic thinkers when he talked with the Stoics and Epicureans at Athens (Acts 17)—Epimenides ("in Him we live and move and exist") and Aratus ("we also are His children").[38] Elsewhere Paul boldly

---

[38] For further discussion of Paul's Mars Hill speech and its relevance for Christians today, see Paul Copan and Kenneth D. Litwak, The Gospel in the Marketplace of Ideas (Downers Grove, IL: IVP Academic, 2014).

appropriated the Stoic term for self-sufficiency (*autarkēs*—not needing favorable external circumstances to be content), although he presents himself as Christ-sufficient (Phil 4:11, 13). Antony Flew, the atheist philosopher-turned-deist, affirmed that Paul was "a highly educated man"—a "first-class intellectual" with "an outstanding philosophical mind."[39]

New Testament scholar N.T. Wright observes that in Paul's day, religion was associated with private piety, which helped keep society running smoothly. Religion didn't threaten the public order. Philosophy, however, *would* be a threat—recall the trial of Socrates. The "philosophy" of the Christian faith presented the convention-shattering metaphysical prospect of an in-breaking divine reality, embodied in Jesus of Nazareth. It demanded a radical new ethic. It called together a new community that disregarded conventional cultural and social boundaries. Paul, Wright affirms, could properly be called a "Jewish philosopher" who challenged the thought-forms of his day and advocated a new way of life. He appeared to be starting more a "new school of philosophy than

---

[39] These descriptions are found in Antony Flew, There Is a God (New York: HarperOne, 2009), 185-86; Antony Flew with Gary Habermas, "My Pilgrimage from Atheism to Theism," Philosophia Christi 6, no.2 (2004): 208; Antony Flew in Did the Resurrection Happen?, ed. David Baggett (Downers Grove, IL: InterVarsity Press, 2009), 57.

a type of religion."[40] And at the heart of Paul's philosophy is Jesus, the crucified and risen Messiah and Lord *(kyrios)* of the world. So, Paul taught, if Jesus is the key to finding all the treasures of wisdom and knowledge and if he is placed at the center of the picture, all our aspirations "after wisdom and right living will fit together" and allow us to catch other glimpses of truth, whatever their source.[41] The Christian faith and philosophy are very much in harmony.

SIN, REASON AND THE IMAGE OF GOD

The church father Tertullian famously asked, "What does Athens have to do with Jerusalem?"—in other words, what does philosophy have to do with the Christian faith? Tertullian claimed to be content with the Porch of Solomon, where Jesus regularly taught. Tertullian took the view, "Don't give me philosophy; just give me Jesus." He insisted: "I believe because it is foolish."[42] Actually, Tertullian did his share of borrowing from philosophy—from the Stoics, Aristotle

---

40 N.T. Wright, Paul and the Faithfulness of God (Minneapolis: Fortress, 2013), 203.

41 Ibid., 1382.

42 Tertullian, Prescription of Heretics 7.9; Tertullian, On the Flesh of Christ 5.4.

and other philosophers. Ironically, as much as he claimed to follow Jesus, he could have benefited from the tools of philosophy—not to mention further biblical study. In fact, he believed that only the *physical* is real and concluded that God must be a physical being. Cyprian—another North African church father—followed him in this error. A century later, Ambrose and Augustine—both of whom embraced a Christianized Neoplatonic philosophy—would overthrow this theological mistake.

Many accuse Martin Luther of being antireason—after all, he called reason a "whore." He advocated a "theology of the cross" *(theologia cruces),* exulting in a suffering God who manifests himself most evidently in the self-humiliation of the crucified Christ. By contrast, he denounced those self-confident "theologians of glory" with all of their sophistic, abstract proofs for God; they only obscured the cross and the gospel.

Actually, Luther would have been quite sympathetic to a book promoting the task of philosophy for Christians. Luther did use blustery rhetoric against scholastic philosophers like Aquinas and his ilk, who relied too much on Aristotle or on particular philosophical constructs imposed on Scripture. For Luther, though, the problem was not with philosophy, reason or metaphysics per se, but with any philosophy that was not shaped by Christ and the cross-event. Luther defended himself at the Diet of Worms by calling on his detractors to show—either from Scripture or "from evident reason"—how he was in error. Also, in the spirit of Augustine, Luther aligned himself considerably less with Aristotle than with Plato. Further, he would say of Cicero that he was "the best philosopher, for he felt that the soul is immortal. He wrote the best on natural, moral and rational philosophy. He is a valuable man, reading with judgment and able to express himself well.... I hope God will forgive such men as Cicero their sins."[43] Although the Scriptures teach the immortality of the body, not the soul, Luther spoke admiringly of this pagan philosopher.

Luther's fellow Reformer John Calvin was more evidently sympathetic to the pursuit of philosophy. He commented on the warning in Colossians 2:8 against philosophizing according to human tradition: "As many have mistakenly imagined that Paul here condemns philosophy, we must define what he means by that word." Of course, what Paul actually opposes is "everything that men contrive of themselves when wishing to be wise in their own understanding—and that not without the specious pretext of reason and apparent probability."[44]

---

[43] Cited in Preserved Smith, The Life and Letters of Martin Luther (Boston: Houghton Mifflin, 1911), 342.

[44] John Calvin, The Epistles of Paul the Apostle to the Galatians, Ephesians, Philippians, and Colossians, trans. T.H.L. Parker, ed. David W. Torrance and Thomas F. Torrance (Grand Rapids: Eerdmans, 1965), 329.

These Reformers believed that philosophy can aid a person's faith. Yet, following Paul, they were also well aware that minds can be darkened and that reason can be directed toward selfcentered ends. Aldous Huxley—noted for the novel *Brave New World* and the neologism "agnostic"—acknowledged that his own motives for coming up with a philosophy of meaninglessness were to justify his pursuit of sexual freedom.[45]

> Take my intellect and use Ev'ry power as Thou shalt choose.
>
> Francis Ridley Havergal

Obviously, suspect motives don't disprove atheism or any other philosophy. They do, however, illustrate what Merold Westphal has called "the law of inverse rationality." He describes the law this way: "The ability of human thought to be undistorted by sinful desire is inversely proportional to the existential import of the subject matter."[46] The less a matter cuts to the core of my being—my humanity—the less likely it is to distort my reasoning. So, for instance, my thinking

---

45 Aldous Huxley, Ends and Means (London: Chatto and Windus, 1969), 270, 273.

46 Merold Westphal, "Taking St. Paul Seriously," in Christian Philosophy, ed. Thomas P. Flint (Notre Dame: University Press, 1990), 205.

is not very likely to be distorted when I perceive a yellow warbler in a branch just outside my window, which leads me to conclude that I am being appeared to warblerly. However, the closer the topic comes to the core of my being—moral choices, guilt, shame, ultimate authority, personal autonomy—the greater the tendency to "subordinate truth to other values."[47] The noetic influence of sin—the impact of sin on the mind—is bound to affect our philosophizing. While the laws of logic are neutral, the use of reason is not. Reason can be marshaled in rebellion against God to suppress the truth and protect human autonomy from divine interference.

On the other hand, God's Spirit can and does use reason and arguments—including reasons for God's existence or for the bodily resurrection of Jesus—to bring people to the truth. After all, he uses personal crises, crushing guilt, the fear of death or a loving believer to awaken people to their need to be reconciled to God. Why not philosophical reasons to lead people to the truth? Reason, we've seen, is a gift from God for all humanity. Used properly, whether to write a logic textbook or to build bridges and skyscrapers, reason expresses the divine image within us. And God has often used reason to persuade inquiring minds of the truth of the Christian faith.

---

[47] Ibid.

4

THINKING ABOUT GOD

A little philosophy inclineth man's mind to atheism; but depth in philosophy bringeth men's minds about to religion.

FRANCIS BACON, *ESSAYS*

***

Philosophy includes metaphysics—the study of ultimate reality. One inescapable metaphysical topic is God—the maximally great being, the being than which nothing greater exists, the being worthy of worship. As we reflect on God, particularly as revealed in Jesus of Nazareth (Jn 14:9), we come up against a couple of sticking points: the influences of negative theology and Greek philosophy on our theology.

Some Christian thinkers and traditions have insisted that we only know about God by *negation*—knowledge of what God is *not* ("God is not foolish" or "God is not hateful"). This kind of theology is sometimes called negative or apophatic theology. As Thomas Aquinas put it, "We cannot know what God is, but only what

He is not."[48] While God's ways are certainly higher than our ways, negative theology doesn't seem to capture what Scripture actually shows—namely, that God reveals himself so that we may know him. God presents us with positive (or cataphatic) knowledge of himself. We can know that God *is* love because Jesus laid down his life for us; in response, we can lay down our lives out of love for others (1 Jn 3:16). We most clearly see who God is through Jesus his Son, who faithfully represents him (Col 1:15; Heb 1:3). Of course, we cannot know God exhaustively, but we can still know him truly. As theologian Colin Gunton observed, the irony of negative theology is that, if it's true, the God who reveals himself in the Bible turns out to be a God who can't be known as he is.[49] Is it really true that the negative attributes of God (that he is not foolish, or not hateful) are *more true* of him than the positive ones (that he is wise and loving)? And can we truly separate God's selfrevealing actions in the world from his actual being?

The second sticking point is this: sometimes Christian philosophy about God has sounded more like Greek

---

48 Thomas Aquinas, Summa Theologica Ia.3, in The Basic Writings of St. Thomas Aquinas, vol.1, trans. and ed. Anton C. Pegis (Indianapolis: Hackett, 1997), 25.

49 See Colin E. Gunton, Act and Being: Towards a Theology of the Divine Attributes (Grand Rapids: Eerdmans, 2003).

philosophy. We don't have to dispute that philosophy—Greek or otherwise—can offer helpful categories, terms and classifications. For example, Aristotle's categories about how a thing *is* can be very useful. Aristotle taught that a thing *is,* first, a substance—something that subsists, or exists, on its own (a tree or a person, for instance). It can also have certain properties (such as brownness or hardness), or it can exist in relation to other substances.[50] When it comes to formulating the doctrine of the Trinity or the incarnation, the categories of *substance* and *relation* greatly assist us. Many of these philosophical terms and categories have served Christians well, providing a theological vocabulary, a conceptual grid and a means of better grasping and communicating the coherence of Christian doctrine. Such doctrinal clarity has guided Christians in worshiping God not only in spirit and but also in truth.

That said, the theological historian Jaroslav Pelikan has noted that two Greek doctrines—divine immutability (unchangeability) and the immortality of the soul—have slipped into accepted Christian doctrine. The question of God's absolute immutability brings us to the august tradition of "classical theism" held by

---

50 See Aristotle's Categories as well as Porphyry's Isagoge ("Introduction"), which expounds on Aristotle's categories (substance, quality, quantity, relation, action, passion, place, time, position and possession).

Augustine, Anselm and Aquinas. By contrast, philosophers like Alvin Plantinga and Richard Swinburne hold to "theistic personalism." They start with God as a personal being, which they believe better reflects the teaching of Scripture; the biblical God who creates and becomes incarnate seems to them quite unlike the seemingly impersonal God of classical theism.[51]

Divine immutability in biblical terms has to do with God's constancy of character and faithfulness to his promises. However, according the Greek philosophical understanding, any change in God—however minute—is impossible. This concept of God was likely the result of philosophers attempting to distance the Ultimate Reality from the erratic, petty, passionate, envying finite deities in the Olympian pantheon. What was the result? Rather than beginning with Scripture's view of God's constancy while affirming his rich personhood and dynamic relationality, many theologians have taken for granted the Greek philosophical view, that any change in God would imply a move toward either perfection or imperfection. And a God who is wrathful might appear too much like the capricious pagan deities.

---

51 Classical theism's position on God includes simplicity (God's existence is identical to his essence; God has no "parts"), eternity (God is timeless or "outside of" time), impassibility (God cannot suffer or be touched by, say, human misery), immutability (God is absolutely without change) and pure actuality (God is without potentiality).

But can't some changes in God be neutral, or even fall within a certain range of goodness? Consider that without the universe, God is *not* the Creator. Yet with God's creative declaration—"Let there be light!"—he *becomes* the Creator, even though he intended this from eternity. Doesn't God acquire the new quality of being Creator—what some call a "relative attribute"? Or isn't it true that the Son of God was *not incarnate* in 500 BC but *becomes incarnate* around 5 BC—in the "fullness of time" (Gal 4:4)? It seems that Scripture reveals a God who acquires new characteristics or properties as he creates, redeems and engages with the world. Becoming Creator and becoming incarnate are noteworthy changes in the life of God, though without diminishing his greatness, his essential character or the covenant faithfulness to his promises. Because he is just, God's wrath is not capricious; rather, it flows from his goodness and love. Yet he is a dynamic, personal, history-engaging, acting God—not some static, abstract, impersonal principle, "Absolute," or the "Ground of all being." The pedigree of classical theism notwithstanding, it does seem as though Pelikan has a point.

Further, *the immortality of the soul* is a very Greek doctrine that many Christians have absorbed. But the notion that we simply "die and go to heaven"—end of story—is not biblical at all. Early Christian thinkers generally distanced themselves from the Platonic doctrine of the soul's pre-existence—Augustine held that view when he wrote the *Confessions* (ca. 400) but later rejected it. Christian creeds have always affirmed "the resurrection of the body and the life everlasting." Indeed, human immortality in Scripture is always connected to the *resurrection of the body*—the final imperishable condition of a transformed physicality in the new heavens and new earth. While philosophical categories and definitions can guide our thinking about God, dangers also lurk, and we must constantly return to the Scriptures as our shaping norm for sound doctrine.

As we reflect on the Christian faith and the history of philosophy we don't want to go as far as Blaise Pascal, who claimed that the God of Abraham, Isaac and Jacob isn't the God of the philosophers and scholars. He still makes an important point. Pascal himself had a life-altering, "night of fire" conversion—a night that filled him with indescribable joy and peace. It was a powerful encounter with a personal God, not some abstract, remote Unmoved Mover, or the Absolute from Greek philosophy. While some overlap exists between philosophical conceptions of God (Greek and otherwise) as self-existent being or the architect of the universe, there is more. The God and Father of our Lord Jesus Christ draws near to us through his Son, loves his enemies, is intimately involved with our lives, humbles himself by becoming incarnate and gives himself to redeem us.

THE CONCEPT OF GOD

Critics have often challenged the coherence of the concept of a maximally great and worship-worthy being "than which nothing greater can be conceived," as Anselm put it. Even some theologians challenge this seemingly philosophy-inspired "perfectbeing theology." However, the Scriptures do contain similar language: "LORD, who is like you?" (Ps 35:10; 89:8; 113:5).

> Great are You, O Lord, and greatly to be praised; great is Your power, and of Your wisdom there is no end.
>
> Augustine, *Confessions*

Philosophers have certainly raised questions about greatestconceivable-being theology. Isn't the very idea of "necessary existence" a contradiction in terms, as Immanuel Kant insisted? Isn't the notion of a disembodied personal being like God incoherent—that is, an earless, eyeless spirit perceiving what is happening in the physical world? Is God "eternal"—is he in "complete, simultaneous and perfect possession of everlasting life," as Boethius claimed? Or is God timeless, but entered into time at creation? Does divine omnipotence mean that God can do literally anything—like changing the past or making square circles? Does the question "Can God make a stone so big that he cannot lift it?"—called the "stone paradox"—have any validity?

Such philosophical questions about God have received a great deal of attention,[52] and Christian philosophers have been at the forefront of robustly and creatively defending the coherence of Christian theism. The tools of philosophy shed light on what "nothing is impossible with God" means. They help to show that the ability to lift unliftable stones is nonsensical—like creating square circles or changing past events—*no* power can accomplish such things.

As we've noted, trained philosophers are doing excellent work in theology. Analytic theology is a thriving field, and there is much more room for exploration. Yes, analytic theology is always a work in progress; doctrinal models of the Trinity, incarnation or atonement will continue to be tested by the Scriptures and refined by the tools of philosophy, and some models will need some or even serious revision. Others will need to be discarded altogether.

But such philosophical engagement with Christian doctrines offers a range of potential theories showing that Christian doctrine is far from incoherent or

---

[52] For starters, see Paul Copan, Loving Wisdom: Christian Philosophy of Religion (St Louis: Chalice Press, 2007); Chad Meister and Paul Copan, eds., The Routledge Companion to Philosophy of Religion, 2nd ed. (London: Routledge, 2012).

self-contradictory. Furthermore, the Christian philosopher can often *thank* critics for their arguments aimed at exposing theism's problems. These criticisms can assist us in clarifying what, say, *omniscience, omnipotence,* or *timelessness* mean in order to tighten our arguments and finetune these concepts. Theistic philosophers have defended different perspectives on these divine attributes; so if critics turn out to be correct about one particular understanding of a certain attribute, the theist has recourse to alternative explanations.

Christians who say "Don't give me philosophy; just give me Jesus" have already benefited from the use of philosophical terms and categories from church history to faithfully express foundational orthodox doctrines. The Trinity—the Christian doctrine that God is three persons *(personae)* who share one substance *(substantia)*—is a case in point. Many theologians and philosophers have noted that the Christian formulation of God as a Trinity has actually shaped the modern—some might say "Western"—understanding of personhood, which we primarily apply to human beings. This discourse has has had a more wideranging effect as well. A broader, global appreciation for human rights is reflected in the United Nations Universal Declaration of Human Rights (1948)—a document drafted primarily by Christians. We ought to thank God for philosophically-minded Christians across the ages who have helped the church clarify, defend and preserve sound doctrine.

THE EXPLANATORY FRUITFULNESS OF GOD

Though not a theist, the philosopher Sir Anthony Kenny wrote about the inspiration brought about by the idea of God.

> If there is no God, then God is incalculably the greatest single creation of the human imagination. No other creation of the imagination has been so fertile of ideas, so great an inspiration to philosophy, to literature, to painting, sculpture, architecture, and drama. Set beside the idea of God, the most original inventions of mathematicians and the most unforgettable characters in drama are minor products of the imagination: Hamlet and the square root of minus one pale into insignificance by comparison.[53]

Besides the fertile idea of God, we should also consider God's robust explanatory power. Alvin Plantinga says that theism "offers suggestions for answers to a wide range of otherwise intractable questions."[54] The existence of consciousness, beauty,

---

[53] Anthony Kenny, Faith and Philosophy (New York: Columbia University Press, 1983), 59.

[54] Alvin Plantinga, "Natural Theology," in Companion to Metaphysics, ed. Jaegwon Kim and Ernest Sosa (Oxford, UK: Blackwell, 1995), 347.

free will, personhood, rationality, duties and human value—not to mention the beginning and fine-tuning of the universe and existence of life itself—are hardly surprising if a good, personal, rational, creative, powerful and wise God exists. Conversely, these phenomena are quite startling if they are the result of deterministic, valueless, nonconscious and nonrational material processes.

> The world is charged with the grandeur of God.
>
> Gerard Manley Hopkins, "God's Grandeur"

We should, of course, assess worldviews and perspectives sympathetically and fair-mindedly. If we are critical of another philosophy, we should always imagine an adherent of that philosophy in our audience, or looking over our shoulder as we write. Even so, we should consider the metaphysical "furniture" contained within any given worldview to help us scrutinize it. This will help us judge how well worldviews anticipate the existence or emergence of important phenomena in the world and in human experience.

Take naturalism, for instance. Naturalism has three fundamental tenets: the physical world is the sum total of reality *(metaphysics);* all causes are deterministic *(etiology);* and all knowledge comes through science *(epistemology).* Naturalism requires that consciousness emerged from nonconscious matter;

rationality is the product of nonrational processes; personal action is the result of deterministic processes; alleged moral duties and the notion of human dignity are the outcome of valueless processes; natural beauty is the product of mindless material forces; the universe's beginning came from nothing (being came from nonbeing); the earth's amazing fine-tuning is the result of unguided physical processes; biological life emerged—against astonishing odds—from nonliving matter.

Surely a self-sufficient, self-existent, intelligent, powerful, free, rational, supremely valuable, creative, conscious being makes better sense of all these phenomena. If such a being should choose to create, we would expect indications of his presence and workmanship: a finite and finely-tuned universe, life, consciousness, rationality, free will, human value and dignity, beauty and the like. The "furniture" of theism offers a far more natural fit for these phenomena than naturalism.

Naturalists themselves frequently declare the glory of God when they acknowledge how ill-equipped naturalism is to explain these phenomena. They plainly admit how strange it is that soggy grey matter should produce technicolor subjective experience (Colin McGinn), that agency should emerge from chemicals, bone and muscle movements (Thomas Nagel), or that there is something rather than nothing (Derek Parfit). These admissions by naturalists actually help reinforce the case for belief in God. Naturalist John Searle wonders: "There is exactly one overriding question in contemporary philosophy.... How do we fit in? ... How can we square this self-conception of ourselves as mindful, meaning-creating, free, rational, etc., agents with a universe that consists entirely of mindless, meaningless, unfree, nonrational, brute physical particles?"[55] Given such conundrums, the idea of God sounds much more intellectually inviting and persuasive.[56]

MORE THAN RATIONAL REASONS

The Christian faith makes good philosophical sense. But there's more: it can be lived out in everyday life, and it meets our deepest needs and fulfills our innermost longings.

All things being equal, if we have to choose between a worldview that can be consistently lived out and one that cannot, it is intuitively fitting to go with the former. The Scottish skeptic David Hume denied that a self exists; after all, such a thing is unobservable. "You" are simply a changing bundle of properties, he argued—much like a classical Buddhist view. Thomas

---

55 John R. Searle, Freedom and Neurobiology (New York: Columbia University Press, 2007), 4.

56 See Paul Copan, "The Naturalists Are Telling the Glory of God," in Philosophy and the Christian Worldview, ed. David Werther and Mark D. Linville (New York: Continuum, 2012).

Reid, a fellow Scot and a philosopher of commonsense realism, responded to Hume with wry humor: what "a most amazing discovery" that Hume's *Treatise of Human Nature* had no author at all and that its ideas organized themselves through various "associations and attractions."[57] Reid insisted that, in the absence of strong reasons to the contrary, we should embrace what seems inescapable and obvious to our everyday experience. Why reject the self's existence when it seems so commonsensical and fundamental to interpreting reality? Why follow Hume in embracing what seems so utterly counterintuitive to our experience?

When our philosophy of life runs contrary to the way the world works, maybe it's time to find a new one. Hume himself admitted that his ivory tower philosophy couldn't be lived out in everyday life—a "most deplorable condition imaginable" that plunged him into "deepest darkness." The best he could do to shake off the "philosophical melancholy and delirium" was to enjoy dinner and a game of backgammon with friends.[58] Thankfully, the Christian philosopher isn't

---

57 Thomas Reid, An Inquiry into the Human Mind: On the Principles of Common Sense, 4th ed., ed. Derek R. Brookes (Edinburgh: University of Edinburgh Press, 1997), 2.6.13-14, 35.

58 David Hume, A Treatise of Human Nature, ed. L.A. Selby-Bigge (Oxford, UK: Clarendon, 1740; repr. 1888), 1.4.7, 269.

forced to choose between philosophical ideals and everyday life.

> Death is the abyss.... We try to do everything we can to create within us a sense that death is not near, that it can be ignored, that ultimate issues are mists far beyond the horizon.
>
> Thomas Morris, *Making Sense of It All*

Besides rational reasons, Christian theism offers practical reasons for personally embracing God. We are more than thinking beings. Pascal spoke of having "reasons of the heart," and we would be foolish to ignore these interior reasons since we are relational, spiritual, emotional and moral beings. We have a fear of death and we long for immortality—or at least to be connected to something that will outlive us. We possess deep longings for security—for relationships and a sense of belonging. We also long for significance, which comes through having a purpose. These yearnings are ultimately satisfied through God in Christ, through whom each of us can have ultimate security through a relationship with God. And my longing for ultimate significance comes through living out a God-given purpose for my life as a human being and as a unique individual. In God we have both union and uniqueness, security and significance, relationship and rationale in life.

Other interior reasons for seeking transcendent help have to do with our feelings of guilt and shame. We are "miserable offenders" of our own professed moral standards. And if we are even minimally self-aware, we are profoundly conscious of our own deep moral inadequacy—that a moral gap exists between us and the ideal. To be clear, the *experience* of guilt doesn't necessarily indicate *objective* guilt: we could feel guilty for faulty reasons, or we may not feel guilty when we truly *are.* Similarly, the fact that we have deep longings doesn't mean they will be fulfilled. But it would be strange for us to be hungry or thirsty if no food or water existed. Without God these longings seem strange and out of place. But our yearnings for transcendence make plenty of sense if God has set eternity in our hearts (Eccles 3:11). In the gospel of Christ, both the loftiest questions of our intellects and deepest desires of our souls find a resting place.

ATHEISM, AGNOSTICISM AND DIVINE HIDDENNESS

Michael Scriven has insisted that atheism needs no defense. In the absence of any evidence for God's existence, atheism is the default position.[59] The problem with this line of reasoning is that we could replace "atheism" with "agnosticism" without any clear

---

[59] Michael Scriven, Primary Philosophy (New York: McGraw-Hill, 1966), 102.

differentiation between the two. Some atheists get a bit slippery or just plain sloppy here. Traditionally, atheism—the "no God" position—claims that God does *not* exist. This is *dis* belief (a rejection of belief in God). It is not mere *un* belief (lack of belief in God)—a position the agnostic could readily claim. The atheist's knowledge-claim that God does not exist calls for justification—not just hanging back and waiting to hear and assess the theist's case *for* God. To assume Scriven's stance is wrongheaded.

Indeed, being a real atheist is just plain tough. It requires more than just debunking arguments for God's existence. An agnostic could do this without becoming an atheist. The atheist's task is considerably more challenging: she has to give reasons why God does not or cannot exist.

What about the agnostic—the one without knowledge of God's existence? The agnostic view comes in at least two varieties. "Regular" or "ordinary" agnostics would like to know whether God exists but claim to lack sufficient evidence. By contrast, "resistant"—some might say "ornery"—agnostics insist that they don't know whether God exists. But, they add, *"You can't know either!"* Notice that resistant agnostics are also making a knowledge claim that stands in need of justification. They may really not know whether God exists, but why insist that others can't know either? How do they know that knowledge of God is beyond *everyone's* ken? Surely they need to do more than just assert such a claim.

And things get thorny for regular agnostics too. Scripture enjoins us to seek God with all our hearts so that we may find him (Jer 29:13). But frankly, a lot of agnostics are more like "apatheists": they don't know whether God exists because they just don't care to look for him. But they aren't off the epistemological or metaphysical hook. Not all ignorance is innocent. There can be a *culpable* ignorance, much like when we don't know the speed limit. When the state trooper pulls us over, our ignorance of the speed limit is no excuse. And we can be culpably ignorant about cosmic matters, too. There can be things we ought to know but haven't bothered to search out with patience, determination and humility. People can spend their lives pursuing trivialities and diversions and never devote even a few hours to a serious inquiry into the "God question."

While evidence for God has its place, God doesn't want to be known as the mere object of philosophical musings. The demons are monotheists, but their right belief is still inadequate (Jas 2:19). The God and Father of our Lord Jesus Christ desires to be known personally—by filial knowers—as *my* Lord and *my* God, as "God, whose I am, and whom I serve" (Acts 27:23 AV). To be without this knowledge—which Jesus calls "eternal life"—is to be epistemologically deficient. Wisdom begins with the fear of the Lord. So why should God humor the skeptic who demands signs and wonders when the skeptic hasn't the remotest interest in bending the knee to God? As Søren

Kierkegaard insisted to the nominal Danish Lutherans around him, God is to be embraced with "passionate inwardness" rather than sheer cool objectivity.[60] While *what* we believe is critical, *how* we believe is vital as well.

Evidence can only bring us so far, and we must exert our will to act on what we know. Socrates claimed that to truly know something means to act on that belief. The Scriptures, though, are more in tune with human experience. Contrary to Socrates's claim, intellectual understanding—like knowing that smoking and eating junk food are bad for us—does not necessarily lead us to stop these habits. We can know the good we ought to do but still sin by failing to carry it out (Jas 4:17). Believing that God exists is certainly a start, but true faith includes a confident trust that God rewards those who diligently seek him (Heb 11:6).

Evidential or intellectual knowledge is only one type of knowledge, and it doesn't necessarily lead to action. Scripture routinely emphasizes the importance of *personal* knowledge—an "I-Thou," relational knowledge of both God and others. More broadly speaking, we can have *experiential* or "lived" knowledge that goes beyond textbook learning to real life. Scripture

---

60 Søren Kierkegaard, Concluding Unscientific Postscript, trans. David Swenson and Walter Lowrie, 3rd ed. (Princeton: Princeton University Press, 1974), 182.

emphasizes that proper knowledge is experiential, not merely theoretical. Eternal life is to know God by his Son (Jn 17:3), and this knowledge further involves personally experiencing divine love (Rom 5:5; Eph 3:14-19; 1 Jn 4:16).

For a long time philosopher Mortimer Adler resisted belief even though he was fully convinced of the intellectual soundness of the Christian faith, until his late-life conversion on a hospital bed. He confessed that philosophical reasoning in itself cannot bring us into relationship with God: "I simply did not wish to exercise a will to believe." He wrote:

> The soundest rational argument for God's existence could only carry us to the edge of the chasm that separated the philosophical affirmation of God's existence from the religious belief in God. What is usually called "a leap of faith" is needed to carry anyone across the chasm. But the leap of faith is usually misunderstood as having insufficient reasons for affirming God's existence to a state of greater certitude in that affirmation. That is not the case. The leap of faith consists in going from the conclusion of a merely philosophical theology to a religious belief in a God that has revealed himself as a loving, just and merciful

Creator of the cosmos, a God to be loved, worshiped and prayed to.[61]

For Adler, this was no "blind leap." It was a well-informed personal embrace of God.

If God exists, what attitude should we adopt? We should adopt a humble stance: *Am I willing to receive whatever light God gives me in whatever way he chooses?* We should avoid a demanding stance that insists that God perform signs and wonders before we agree to believe. This "ultimatum model" makes us the final authority. But why should God bother making himself known to the proud—or the apathetic, or the halfhearted? Instead, he reveals himself to wholehearted seekers (Jer 29:13). As Pascal put it, God is

> willing to appear openly to those who seek Him with all their heart, and to be hidden from those who flee from Him with all their heart, He so regulates the knowledge of Himself that He has given signs of Himself, visible to those who seek Him, and not to those who seek Him not. There is enough light for those who only desire to see,

---

[61] Mortimer Adler, "A Philosopher's Religious Faith," in *Philosophers Who Believe*, ed. Kelly James Clark (Downers Grove, IL: InterVarsity Press, 1993), 209, 215.

and enough obscurity for those who have a contrary disposition.[62]

---

[62] Blaise Pascal, Pensées, trans. W.F. Trotter, Harvard Library 48 (New York: P.F. Collier and Son, 1910), no.430, 144.

PART TWO

HOW TO STUDY PHILOSOPHY

5

VIRTUOUS PHILOSOPHY

MORAL VIRTUES: HUMILITY, KINDNESS, CHARITY

In the philosophy guild, the vices of arrogance, ruthlessness and antagonism can eclipse key moral virtues like humility, kindness and charity. Philosopher Richard Taylor openly confessed his own pride:

> Most of my life was foolishly spent, and parts of it I can only recall with shame. For one thing, I was under the illusion that happiness is the reward of success and recognition, which are really opiates. Approving audiences, distinguished academic chairs, rapid advancement, even the taste of fame—these are heady things, but they are blinding. My eyes began to open when my self-centredness and disdain for basic decencies nearly led to my moral and intellectual ruin.[63]

---

63 Keith Seddon, "Interview with Richard Taylor," The Philosopher: Journal of the Philosophical Society of England (November 1992): 3-4.

Alas, those who should be the most humble and gracious philosophers of all—professing Christ-followers—are not immune. Christian philosophers are not always above such pettinesses as, for instance, insisting that their name appear first on the cover of a coedited book, even when they haven't done the lion's share of the work.

Pride is a temptation for both the seasoned philosopher and the novice. How quickly the beginning philosophy student becomes a self-described "philosopher"! My philosophy professor Stuart Hackett—a model of modesty—called himself "a *student* of philosophy." To his mind, the term "philosopher" was better suited for the likes of Aristotle or Aquinas.

In Plato's *Gorgias* dialogue, Socrates acknowledges his own ignorance and confusion. This admission can lead, Plato reasoned, first to honest opinions, and then eventually to knowledge. Recognizing our ignorance should be a starting point not only for learning, but also for prayerful dependence on the Lord: "What do you have that you did not receive? And if you did receive it, why do you boast as if you had not received it?" (1 Cor 4:7). True humility entails being in touch with reality—the reality of our weakness and ignorance as well as any philosophical endowments from on high. By contrast, to be prideful is to be out of touch with reality. Pride becomes our own self-advertising campaign—an effort to look better than we really are. One temptation for philosophers is to give the impression that we are better-read and better-informed than we really are. Or we may act as though the skills and strengths we possess are not gifts from God.

Philosophizing according to the pattern of Jesus will certainly reject sloppy thinking and slipshod arguments, but it still involves *love*—particularly in the form of kindness and graciousness. Heavenly wisdom is "gentle," and Scripture enjoins us to give a reason for our inner hope with gentleness and respect (Jas 3:17; 1 Pet 3:15). And again: "The Lord's servant must not be quarrelsome but must be kind to everyone" (2 Tim 2:24 NIV). Let those who take pride in proving others wrong stay away from professional philosophy.

Practicing philosophy in the way of Jesus, for instance, requires that professors never publicly dismantle a graduate student's paper at a conference. Rather, the professor should catch the student in the hallway or send a note to offer constructive criticism. And while Christian philosophers can develop fine arguments for God's existence or the rationality of the Christian faith, Thomas Senor says that we can best represent Christ by "demonstrating a spirit of charity toward our colleagues, and by showing respect and kindness particularly to those in our discipline who lack power and prestige. May they know we are Christians ... by our helpfulness and our intellectual humility."[64] And—who knows?—Jesus might say to us at the final judgment, "I was a young graduate student in philosophy and you offered me encouragement. I was standing alone at a philosophy conference and you bought me a cup of coffee. I wrote a paper and you collaborated with me to help get it published."

Christian philosophy also involves *charity*—a generosity of spirit toward others. This means giving those who disagree with us the benefit of the doubt by putting their contrary arguments in the best possible light. It means refusing to caricature others' views for easy dismantling. We must patiently work through an argument by suggesting, drawing out and responding to the most plausible lines of reasoning we can find in their argument. "When my detractor asserts that P, it seems to me that he could mean either X, Y or Z."

Being uncharitable mars civil discourse and cheapens philosophical discussion. Christ calls us both to speak and receive the truth in love—to speak charitably and graciously to others and to humbly receive their criticism through conversations, correspondence, debates, rejoinders and surrejoinders in published journal articles. This spirit serves as a kind of

---

64 Thomas Senor, "Still More Advice to Christians in Philosophy," Logoi, University of Notre Dame's Center for Philosophy of Religion (Spring 2015): 8.

philosophical sandpaper by which the hard edges of our ideas and arguments are rounded off and our dull arguments are sharpened. It is also like a philosophical oil that creates a context for courteous exchanges and friendships across the philosophical spectrum.

> He who gives an answer before he hears, it is folly and shame to him.
>
> Proverbs 18:13

Wisdom is the skill of living. If we love wisdom, we'll attend not only to our thinking but to our very lives: "You yourselves are our letter, written on our hearts, known and read by everyone" (2 Cor 3:2 NIV). As Paul Moser reminds us, our lives are to be "the personifying evidence of the divine reality."[65] So whether we publish much or little, whether our work is widely admired or falls stillborn from the press, we are still to be a faithful presence wherever God has placed us. We must cultivate the resources and opportunities God has given to us rather than burying them in our discouragement or wounded pride.

---

65 Paul K. Moser, The Elusive God: Reorienting Religious Epistemology (Cambridge, UK: Cambridge University Press, 2008), 2.

INTELLECTUAL VIRTUES: PERSEVERANCE AND COURAGE

As philosophers—particularly Christian ones—we must not only take the moral virtues seriously—we must cultivate the *intellectual* virtues as well. The intellectual virtues are directed toward certain epistemic ends like truth, knowledge, understanding and rationality.[66] The love of truth will naturally involve cultivating intellectual virtues like curiosity, attentiveness, impartiality, open-mindedness, perseverance and courage.

But aren't, say, perseverance and courage *moral* virtues? Yes, they are. When it comes to the pursuit of truth and knowledge, however, a morally bankrupt person can still display certain intellectual virtues. After all, wicked people can know and explain $E=mc^2$ or Newton's laws of motion. Yet even when intellectually virtuous knowers aren't good people, they demonstrate moral virtue when they help their students or their children become better learners and knowers. When they move beyond themselves as individual knowers to assist others in knowing, intellectual virtue spills over into moral virtue.

---

[66] See Jason Baehr, The Inquiring Mind: On Intellectual Virtues & Virtue Epistemology (Oxford: Oxford University Press, 2012).

Just as intellectual virtues shouldn't be confused with moral virtues, neither should they be confused with *natural* or *innate* abilities. Having a photographic memory or a mathematical mind capable of breaking intricate secret codes isn't intellectually virtuous. Intellectual virtue isn't based on natural skills, talents or temperaments or on properly functioning senses and cognitive faculties. Rather, the intellectual virtues are fostered by human agency and intentionality. For example, while our sense of hearing may be functioning properly, it takes time, patience and diligent study to discern the sounds of this or that bird species as we walk through the woods. Also, remember that cultivating these intellectual virtues doesn't guarantee knowledge—warranted true belief. But these intellectual virtues do play a supportive role in the knowing process.

Take the intellectual virtue of perseverance, for example. Philosophy can be a daunting enterprise. When I began studying philosophy in graduate school, I read through Frederick Copleston's magisterial nine-volume *History of Philosophy.* Being new to many of the philosophical concepts Copleston covered, I had to read and reread many lines and paragraphs carefully. I soon realized that zoning out for a paragraph or even a sentence or two meant I would have to read the paragraph or page over again. As I read, I wrote summary thoughts in the margins and looked up unfamiliar words in philosophical dictionaries, and then memorized key terms and their definitions.

In classes and at philosophy conferences, my mind would often swirl as I tried to understand discussions about abstract objects and the ontological argument for God's existence. Yet I knew that driving out the demons of ignorance and self-doubt does not come about except by grit and determination and much trust in the Lord.

Doing philosophy involves hard, careful work. During his studies at St. Deiniol's College in Wales, Catholic philosopher and logician Peter Geach began to probe the work of Thomas Aquinas. He observed just how linguistically self-conscious the "Angelic Doctor" was. How very precise he was when he unpacked the logical and grammatical status of nouns, adjectives, verbs, and particles! Aquinas's fine distinctions would help shed much light on Geach's own intellectual path, which would lead to important contributions to the philosophy of logic. We cannot be mere dabblers if we want to do philosophy well. Philosophy requires perseverance.

I discovered early that [philosophy] is simultaneously the most exciting and frustrating of subjects. It is exciting because it is the broadest of all disciplines.... It is frustrating because its great generality makes it extremely difficult.

Anthony Kenny, *What I Believe*

Another intellectual virtue is courage. This involves pursuing the truth and a deepened understanding of the way things really are, even if doing so flies in the face of dominant philosophical views and risks losing prestige or acceptability in the eyes of our philosophical peers. In the mid-twentieth century, when logical positivism was all the rage, many Christian philosophers were intimidated by the demands of "verificationism." For a statement to be coherent or meaningful, positivists taught, it had to be either *true by definition* (or "analytically" true) or *scientifically* (empirically) *verifiable.* Positivists insisted that religious language like "God is love" or "God created the world" was meaningless, since it can't be empirically verified.

Many Christian intellectuals were cowed into silence by the arbitrary demands of verificationism, while others tried to show how the Christian faith could rise to meet such demands. But like a modern version of the emperor's new clothes, C.E.M. Joad, Karl Popper, W.V.O. Quine and others exposed the fundamental self-contradictions and problems with this view. They pointed out that logical positivism itself is neither true by definition nor empirically verifiable. Is it therefore meaningless? And how could anyone scientifically prove that all knowledge must be scientifically provable? While science does help in the quest for knowledge, it is arbitrary to insist that science is the *only* means for doing so. What about acquiring knowledge through theology, philosophy, art, personal relationships or ethical insight?

What's more, the history of science itself shows that well-established scientific theories often begin not with empirical verification, but with instincts and hunches, personal insight and creative genius. Logical positivism has now gone deservedly extinct, though some of its not-quite-fossilized proponents are still trying to preserve whatever remains of this incoherent notion.

In our philosophizing, we must have the courage to do at least two things: to resist false ideas in our pursuit of knowledge and to pursue philosophy in a distinctively Christian manner.

First, the Christian faith is necessarily committed to resisting what is false and pursuing the truth. If our faith is false—if Christ has not been raised from the dead (1 Cor 15:32)—we ought to abandon it. Indeed, we should reject any worldview that doesn't match up with reality. The Christian faith is a matter of public truth, and its intellectual integrity, explanatory power and rational coherence can be explored by anyone. The pursuit of knowledge requires both embracing true beliefs and rejecting false ones. We cannot do one and not the other. After all, in the attempt to embrace as many true beliefs as possible, a gullible person may believe everything they hear—but this process will include embracing many falsehoods. By contrast, the skeptic's attempt to avoid false beliefs may mean rejecting everything she hears, but this will eliminate many true beliefs.

Second, the Christian faith begins with distinctive and defensible starting points. These include the existence of an omniscient, omnipotent and benevolent triune God; human beings made in his image and endowed with dignity and responsibility; the finitude of the universe; the reality of goodness and its deviation, evil; the rationality, order and knowability of the universe; the possibility—and actuality—of miracles; and, although some Christians would debate this specific point the reality of the self (or soul) that can survive the death of the body—that is, substance dualism. While such beliefs may not be fashionable, we should not abandon them. Church history has its share of intellectual giants who have eloquently defended these views, and we would be unwise to jump ship because of philosophical innovations, fads and naysayers. Let me mention three of these distinctives—the self, miracles and science.

Consider the *soul* or the *self.* J.P. Moreland has written extensively about consciousness and the existence of the soul (or the self); this feature of reality serves as a strong argument for a supremely self-aware spirit being.[67] Yet Moreland has found two related phenomena in the relevant philosophical literature: *hylomania* (a fixation on matter) and *pneumatophobia* (fear of spirit or soul). He observes that many

---

67 See the last chapter of J.P. Moreland, Consciousness and the Existence of God: A Theistic Argument (London: Routledge, 2008).

academic treatments of the mind-body issue are overly dismissive of substance dualism. These critics tend to follow a predictable pattern: they interact with René Descartes's more compartmentalized, nonintegrated version of dualism, reject it and assume their work is done. However, they usually ignore or refuse to address more sophisticated treatments of this view. This shouldn't be surprising, since naturalism has no room for a soul or self.

However, if an embodied soul capable of surviving physical death exists, this would be most significant. For one thing, it would indicate that the physical world is not all there is. It would point us toward a supernatural source—a mind or a soul—that is capable of creating and interacting with the physical world—"this all men speak of as God," Aquinas wrote.[68] Secondly, the self would go a long way toward explaining elements of our human experience. It makes better sense of personal responsibility and free will (the idea that we are responsible for at least some of our moral acts); of the fact that we retain our personal identities even as our bodies change over time; of the unity of our multisensory and mental experiences at any given time; and of our unique subjective or inner experience.

---

68 Thomas Aquinas, Summa Theologica in Introduction to St. Thomas Aquinas, ed. Anton Pegis (New York: Modern Library, 1948), I.2.3.

Yes, there are Christian materialists. Back in 2011 I heard one of them candidly admit that Jesus and Paul were substance dualists. He himself rejected this view since he couldn't imagine himself without his body, although this hasn't been a problem for most of humanity across the ages, let alone Christians. Indeed, God's Son could imagine himself without a body before his incarnation or between his death and resurrection.

Also, this view makes better sense of important Christian doctrines. One of them is the incarnation: God, a spirit being, takes on a human body. Another is the resurrection of the body: a soul would ground personal identity between death and resurrection. The substance dualist doesn't need to deny the ongoing existence of the self between death and resurrection, as some Christian materialists do. The point here is not so much to defend the often maligned and misrepresented position of substance dualism. Rather, if it is a biblical doctrine—if Jesus and Paul really *did* hold this view—then we should too. Indeed we have many intellectual resources to defend it. We do not need to embrace hylomania or live with pneumatophobia.

We can be encouraged that philosophers of mind like Jaegwon Kim, Ned Block, Colin McGinn and John Searle—naturalists all—acknowledge that they have no clue how consciousness and inner experience could emerge from firing neurons and soggy grey matter. Nor do they understand how the mental and physical interact—which, ironically, is one of their stated reasons for rejecting substance dualism!

We should also be courageous when it comes to miracles. What's the big deal if antimiracle proponents think that miracles are no longer intellectually fashionable? How is that even an argument against the philosophical plausibility of miracles? Why accept David Hume's rigged definition of miracles as "violations" of the laws of nature? A miracle occurs precisely when the world is not left to itself. Hume himself presented us with "the problem of induction," which asserts that the invariability of patterns in nature—like the sunrise and sunset—is no guarantee that those patterns will actually continue. Hume can't have it both ways. Is it impossible or is it possible that the laws of nature can be violated? As Tom Morris has pointed out, critics of miracles or of arguments for God's existence tend to invoke Hume and Kant as authorities, but they routinely fail to explain—let alone attempt to show—just what the allegedly devastating argument is. Not surprisingly, various nontheists have criticized Hume for his "abject failure" in this regard.

If God is the originator of the universe, why can't he also be at work *within* it? Why must the Christian bow to naturalistic demands and assumptions? Even if the physical world operates according to general patterns, or laws, why must these laws be inviolable? Even if miracles are highly improbable, why should we assume that, all things being equal, the improbable never occurs? Instead, we can think of natural laws as simple *descriptions* of the way things generally operate—unless some other agent acts upon the world—rather than *prescriptions* of the way everything in the world must necessarily operate. The believing philosopher can shrug off the notion that natural laws are inviolable. If God exists and the universe is open to his action, why couldn't he, say, raise the dead? If God created the universe out of nothing, why would a virgin birth be impossible?

Courage is also in order as we consider the relationship between the Christian faith and science. Christian scholars may be tempted or even pressured to follow the rules of the academy. Christian philosophers, historians or scientists can, for instance, assume a *methodological naturalism*—that is, interpreting events or phenomena in the natural world without reference to God or the miraculous, even though these scholars believe in God and miracles. (Of course, to reject God's existence would be philosophical or metaphysical naturalism, which is markedly different.)

We must not automatically assimilate what is current or fashionable or popular by way of philosophical opinion and procedures; for much of it comports ill with Christian ways of thinking. And ... we must display more Christian self-confidence or courage or boldness. We have a perfect right to our pre-philosophical views: why, therefore, should we

> be intimidated by what the rest of the philosophical world thinks plausible or implausible?
>
> Alvin Plantinga, "Advice to Christian Philosophers"

Up to a point, methodological naturalism can serve as a check against intellectual laziness or evidential sloppiness. Indeed, plenty of theists have resorted to saying "God did it" to plug the gaps of their ignorance about highly unusual or seemingly inexplicable events, only for it to become glaringly apparent that natural processes can easily account for them. We should marshal appropriate support for supernaturalistic interpretations while acknowledging (still divinely engineered) predictable natural processes. Belief in a "God of the gaps"—a God who is there just to explain the things we don't understand—can be just plain lazy.

However, if our methodology squeezes out any room for detecting divine agency or divine intelligence in the world, we are left with a sub-biblical position. Yes, the Christian historian or scientist may be able to keep naturalists at bay by saying, "History (or science) can neither rule out nor show that a miracle occurred." But this often slips into a kind of practical deism: a belief in a detached and uninvolved deity. As a result, we can no longer trace God's miraculous work in the world. In the end we'll only find the best *naturalistic* explanation, instead of the best *overall* explanation. And perhaps we'll no longer stick out our necks in defense of true miracles—events that cannot be explained by natural processes. Thankfully, many scholars have stuck out their necks, such as Craig Keener.[69] Keener has documented hundreds and hundreds of miracle accounts, many with medical authentication and eyewitness testimony. Many of us could give similar miraculous accounts from closer to home.

Shouldn't the Christian historian or scientist seek out the *best* explanation for an event or phenomenon—whether natural or supernatural—rather than just the best *natural* explanation? Don't we live in an open universe, in which God can and does act, rather than a closed one with strictly natural operations? Shouldn't we trust in the power of the Spirit, pray with confidence, and defend eyewitnesses and documented accounts of the supernatural rather than decline to speak of such things in polite academic company?

Of course, we must be wise in the way we go about our task as Christian philosophers and as we engage with those who disagree on these and other topics. My PhD advisor told me not to attempt something earthshaking for my dissertation: after all, I would have to persuade an entire dissertation committee!

---

[69] Craig S. Keener, Miracles: The Credibility of the New Testament Accounts, 2 vols. (Grand Rapids: Baker Academic, 2011).

He suggested I keep my nose to the grindstone, work hard and save any bold work for later. This was sound advice. Likewise, the classroom may not be the right time or place to challenge a professor's atheism. We may first need to do more listening, learning and even cultivating friendships with those who disagree with us. One study I read indicated that many self-proclaimed "secular" professors don't have solid friendships with genuine Christians in the academy, and they certainly resist anything that smacks of a conversion project. In such situations we should engage wisely and graciously, but we should never be ashamed of the gospel or shrink from doing philosophy in a distinctively Christian way.

In sum, we can echo the words of Alvin Plantinga, who urges believing philosophers toward "Christian courage, or boldness, or strength, or perhaps Christian self-confidence. We Christian philosophers must display more faith, more trust in the Lord; we must put on the whole armor of God."[70]

---

[70] Alvin Plantinga, "Advice to Christian Philosophers," Faith and Philosophy 1, no.3 (July 1984): 255.

6

PHILOSOPHY AND COMMUNITY

For those within the philosophy guild itself and students who aspire to belong, philosophy has its hazards and pitfalls. Alvin Plantinga observes:

> We philosophers are brought up to practice our craft in a sort of individualistic, competitive, even egotistical style; there is enormous interest in ranking each other with respect to dialectical and philosophical ability, deciding who is really terrific, who is pretty good, who is OK, who is really lousy and so on....
>
> But all this is flummery, a snare and delusion. Philosophy is not an athletic competition; and success as a Christian philosopher is not an individualistic matter of doing well in the intellectual equivalent of a tennis tournament.[71]

---

[71] Alvin Plantinga, "A Life Partly Lived," in Philosophers Who Believe, ed. Kelly James Clark (Downers Grove, IL: InterVarsity Press, 1993), 79.

Christian philosophers are well-positioned to resist such individualistic patterns by cultivating community with fellow saints in the guild, by loving both their believing and unbelieving colleagues as Christ loved us and by being nourished in the fellowship of the church.

Plantinga's own experience illustrates the rich, life-giving benefit of philosophical community and collegiality. When he taught at Calvin College, he would gather weekly with Nicholas Wolterstorff and others to present and discuss ideas and to offer constructive criticism to sharpen and strengthen these presentations. Plantinga's landmark book *God and Other Minds* (1967) along with his influential *The Nature of Necessity* (1978) emerged from these discussions. Plantinga went on to cofound the Society of Christian Philosophers with its journal *Faith and Philosophy.*

Around 1948 at Oxford, a group of Christian philosophers called the "Metaphysicals" began to meet. This was during the heyday of logical positivism and its repudiation of metaphysics, which in that context meant any belief in God. The meeting of the Oxford Metaphysicals would lead to the publication of Basil Mitchell's important edited book *Faith and Logic* (1957). The same could be said about the Christian community within the Evangelical Philosophical Society, which was launched as a significant professional society in 1998, under William Lane Craig's presidency—along with its new journal, *Philosophia Christi.*

> Reasonable people can disagree with intellectual integrity and even in friendship.
>
> Charles Taliaferro, *Evidence and Faith*

Christian philosophical communities should not exist merely to promote "professional development." We can also worship together, pray together, critique and proofread one another's papers and book manuscripts, mentor graduate students and new colleagues, engage in deep cross-fertilization of ideas, join together in outreach and cultivate rich friendships in Christ.

Of course, the Christian philosophical community is much broader than the academy. We can also benefit from the broader communion of saints—both living ones and the philosophical saints who have gone before us, from Augustine and Aquinas to Blaise Pascal and the Cambridge Platonists to Jonathan Edwards, Søren Kierkegaard and William Alston. Studying their lives and digesting their writings can inspire our faith and shape our craft as we continue on our journeys as philosophically-inclined, Christ-led pilgrims.

But there is more. Christian philosophers can find a community beyond the household of faith. As far as it lies within us, Christian philosophers can and should live at peace with philosophers of all stripes—to enjoy their camaraderie and collegiality, their friendship and their collaboration. How good and how pleasant it is for Christian philosophers to dwell with their non-Christian counterparts in unity!

PHILOSOPHERS AND THE CHURCH

Christian philosophers have often felt out of place in the local church. Yet relationships between philosophers and the local church should be cultivated and encouraged.

First, *the Christian community has much to contribute to the life of the Christian philosopher.* Christian philosophers will naturally gravitate to the guild of other professional philosophers and toward other academics in general. Some of these philosophers, however, will detach themselves—perhaps reluctantly—from ordinary lay Christians, who, though serious about their faith, have not been exposed to the life of the mind. Christian academics may consider them a kind of Christian intellectual proletariat, but there is more to the Christian community than intellectual peers in the faith. True, the philosophical task may not be fully appreciated in certain Christian churches and, let's face it, some churches are engaged in all sorts of nonsense in the name of being relevant and seeker-oriented instead of proclaiming the gospel clearly. Yet where there is sincere devotion to Christ, Christian philosophers should embrace their fellow believers from the heart and engage in reciprocal living—forgiving, accepting and being kind to one another.

Philosopher William Alston attests to the power of a rich church community that helped rekindle his own faith. Those believers helped him to experience the reality of God's presence through the strong bond of love, corporate worship and the practice of spiritual gifts. It was during this time of faith-renewal that he sensed God telling to him to devote his life to philosophy. Alston describes his experience:

> I'm a Christian not because I have been convinced by some impressive arguments: arguments from natural theology for the existence of God, historical arguments concerning the authenticity of the Scriptures or the reliability of the Apostles, or whatever. My coming back was less like seeing that certain premises implied a conclusion than it was like coming to hear some things in music that I hadn't heard before, or having my eyes opened to the significance of things that are going on around me. G.K. Chesterton once wrote: "In the last analysis, the reason why I am a Christian is that the Church is living and not a dead teacher." That pretty much sums it up for me. I'm a Christian because it was in the Christian Church that I came to discover the presence and activity of God in my life.[72]

---

[72] William P. Alston, "A Philosopher's Way Back to Faith," in God and the Philosophers, ed. Thomas V. Morris (Oxford: Oxford University Press, 1993), 27.

Second, *Christian philosophers have much to contribute to the Christian community.* While academics tend to disdain popularizers, Alvin Plantinga charges Christian scholars not to leave their work "buried away in professional journals,"[73] but to make their work available to the broader Christian community to help them grapple with important questions and concerns. "If [Christian philosophers] devote their best efforts to the topics fashionable in the non-Christian philosophical world, they will neglect a crucial and central part of their task as Christian philosophers."[74]

> To be ignorant and simple now—not to meet the enemies on their own ground—would be to throw down our weapons and to betray our uneducated brethren who have, under God, no defense but us against the intellectual attacks of the heathen.
>
> C.S. Lewis, "Learning in War-Time"

One way of doing this is to teach Christians not only to understand their faith better, but also to defend it in the marketplace of ideas. We call this task *apologetics,* which we can define as the art and science of defending the Christian faith.

---

[73] Alvin Plantinga, "Twenty Years' Worth of the SCP," Faith and Philosophy 15 (April 1998): 153.

[74] Alvin Plantinga, "Advice to Christian Philosophers," Faith and Philosophy 1 (July 1984): 255.

Strangely, the agnostic philosopher Paul Draper has been emphatic that philosophers of religion—whether atheists or theists—should *not* engage in apologetics, or in defending their worldview commitment. His reason is that apologists are biased and that they try to justify their own ideas instead of seeking the truth.* Now this is a rather odd apologetic for not doing apologetics. Is Draper's view itself unbiased? Is this recommendation an attempt to justify Draper's own perspective instead seeking the truth? And shouldn't philosophers—in our case, Christian ones—presumably be the *best* equipped to help train believers to defend their views properly? What's more, the Christian faith is dedicated to the truth and it opens itself up to falsification: if Christ hasn't been raised from the dead, our faith is futile and we're out of touch with reality.

[* Nicholas DiDonato, "Paul Draper on 'What Is Philosophy of Religion?'" *Philosophy of Religion* (blog), November 27, 2013, http://philosophyofreligion.org/?p=14582.]

Christian philosophers may engage in defending the Christian faith in different ways. Some are more direct while others are indirect. This is much like two of Oxford's "Inklings" and Christian literary greats—C.S. Lewis, who took the direct approach in defending the Christian faith, and J.R.R. Tolkien, who took a more indirect approach. Lewis wanted to "smuggle theology" into his fantasy stories by way of allegory. The more reserved Tolkien wanted to leave "mere hints" about ultimate matters so that God and angels would only "peep through" his fantasies, though with a rich biblical texture.[75] To whatever degree we do this, we have an obligation to bring our training and gifts to the church, which Christ loves and for which he laid down his life.

---

[75] C.S. Lewis to Sister Penelope, August 9, 1939, in The Collected Letters of C.S. Lewis: Books, Broadcasts, and the War, 1931–1949 (vol.2), ed. Walter Hooper (San Francisco: Harper, 2004), 262-63. See J.R.R. Tolkien to Father Robert Murray, November 4, 1954, in The Letters of J.R.R. Tolkien, ed. Humphrey Carpenter (London: Allen and Unwin, 1981), no.156.

7

DOUBTING WISELY

If you're going to be a doubter, you need to believe your beliefs and doubt your doubts as well as to doubt your beliefs and believe your doubts.

DALLAS WILLARD, *THE ALLURE OF GENTLENESS*

***

A book for Christians who are exploring philosophy should probably include some thoughts on doubt. Philosophy encourages out-of-the-box thinking, and that scares some Christians because, they reason, it could move them toward unbelief. And doesn't James condemn all doubting? He writes that "the one who doubts is like the surf of the sea driven and tossed by the wind ... being a double-minded man, unstable in all his ways" (Jas 1:6-8).

Actually, James is condemning a mindset of divided loyalty between God and the world—a spiritual adultery: "Do you not know that friendship with the world is hostility toward God? ... Cleanse your hands, you sinners; and purify your hearts, you double-minded" (Jas 4:4, 8; see Mt 6:24). Kierkegaard summarizes James's corrective: "Purity of heart is to will one thing." But when Jude exhorts us to "have mercy on some, who are doubting" (Jude 22), he doesn't have James's double-mindedness or divided allegiance in mind. Rather than a rebuke, Jude calls for pastoral care for doubters. One of the seven spiritual works of mercy in the Christian tradition—along with instructing the ignorant and comforting the sorrowful—is *counseling the doubtful.*

Philosophy and doubt often go hand in hand. Descartes embarked on a "skeptical voyage," subjecting every belief he could think of to withering doubt. Why? In order to see which belief could withstand the assault. If it could do so, this meant arriving at a certain, unshakable foundation for knowledge. He concluded that his most severe doubting—which is a form of thinking—entailed his very existence: *Cogito, ergo sum*—"I think; therefore, I am." Descartes' Project Doubt was directed toward a constructive purpose, despite his mixed reviews.

Though not to such an extreme, philosophers typically do a good bit of detached doubting. They raise "what if" or "for the sake of argument" scenarios to clarify and fine-tune concepts and positions. What would it be like to be a bat? Are we simply brains in a vat hooked up to electrodes to create a simulated reality? Would having another person's brain alter my personal identity? Such thought experiments sharpen our understanding of the nature of subjective or inner experience, the trustworthiness of sense perception and the nature of personal identity.

Some in our culture, however, actually commend doubt. Many even celebrate it. This mindset, though, is terribly confused as well as destructive. We should engage in critical thinking, not doubt. Systematic doubt is actually crippling and even corrosive to both virtuous character and a vibrant Christian faith; it can undermine our proper functioning as human beings. Perhaps the following suggestions for Christians interested in philosophy—and hopefully Christians in general—will point the way forward.

First, doubting is quite common to human experience, and the Scriptures offer much comfort, guidance and direction for doubting saints. Psalmists and prophets are filled with doubts and questions. With anguished souls they struggle to discern why God seems so silent and aloof from rampant evil and the prosperity of the wicked (Ps 13; 73; Hab 1:2-4). They are baffled by God's harsh actions. David was angry when God struck Uzzah dead for steadying the tottering Ark of the Covenant (2 Sam 6:1-10). Even John the Baptist, the greatest of the prophets, had doubts about Jesus' messiahship (Lk 7:17-23). Godly Christ-followers have often experienced dark nights of the soul.

Mother Teresa experienced inner pain, torment, darkness and despair. What is less-known is that in 1951, she prayed to share in the sufferings of Christ and to know more fully the sense of abandonment Jesus felt on the cross. "Let me share with You [Jesus] this pain! If my separation from you brings others to you, I am willing with all my heart to suffer all that I suffer ... a very small part, of Jesus' darkness and pain on the earth."[76] God answered this prayer. In the very depths of Jesus' humiliation, anguish and apparent abandonment, God was actually the most present: "God was in Christ reconciling the world to Himself" (2 Cor 5:19). Likewise, God displayed his presence through Mother Teresa's life and work—"something beautiful for God" that was so obvious to the rest of the world, even if not always to Mother Teresa herself. In many ways, this darkness made her better suited to minister to the desperate souls around her.

God doesn't rebuke saints for honest inner struggles, questions and emotions. And even amid their doubt and darkness, they may show forth God's presence through living faithful lives. When we experience such struggles, we are in holy company.

Second, we ought to process our doubts, not suppress them. Insofar as we are able, doubts should be expressed, sorted out and addressed—and this should be done in Christian community. We should seek out godly, thoughtful, seasoned Christians—philosophers included—to assist us and help strengthen our trust in God along the way. Continually giving in to our doubts leads to the prison of cynicism and suspicion, the escape from which is terribly difficult.

---

[76] David Scott, A Revolution of Love: The Meaning of Mother Teresa (Chicago: Loyola, 2010), 156-57.

As a young man in North Africa, Augustine was critical of anti-intellectual church leaders. When they were asked honest questions about what God was doing before he made heaven and earth, these leaders would answer mockingly: "Preparing hell ... for those prying into such deep subjects." Augustine adopted a more honest attitude: "I would rather respond, 'I do not know,' concerning what I do not know rather than say something for which a man inquiring about such profound matters is laughed at while the one giving a false answer is praised."[77] Christian leaders and parents should give the young people entrusted to them ample room to doubt and ask honest questions in open forums and conversations around the supper table. The next generation should receive help in constructively and honestly working through these questions to strengthen their faith so they can embrace it as their own. Great harm comes when we keep our young people in a bubble in an effort to shield them from hard questions, or when we dismiss their struggles and exhort them to "pray harder," "read the Bible" or "just believe."

Theologian Avery Dulles has said that there is a "secret infidel" in every believer's heart—that is, a kind of dialogue takes place between a believer and

---

[77] Confessions, 11.12.14.

an unbeliever in the Christian's mind.[78] We should encourage our youth to have the believer and unbeliever within themselves engage in dialogue with each other. Such intellectually stretching exercises can sharpen their minds and strengthen their faith.

Third, we should recognize that the Christian faith offers ample resources and evidence to assist us. When God enters our lives, we have the Spirit's *internal* confirmation that we are children of God, that we have been accepted before him through Christ and that we can thus approach him with confidence (Rom 8:14-16; Gal 4:5-6; Heb 4:16; 1 Jn 5:13). Related to this are the practical or existential supports for the truth of the gospel. Our deepest longings and needs are met in Christ: overcoming the fear of death, finding ultimate security and significance, and experiencing forgiveness from guilt and relief from shame. Along with this inner evidence, we have ample *external* supports for God's existence, for the historical reliability of the Scriptures, for the historicity of Jesus' resurrection and for the plausibility—and the actual occurrence of—miracles.

This isn't to say we have exhaustive answers (1 Cor 13:12). Often we may have to be content with partial ones; we have to live with certain perplexing questions. We nevertheless have excellent reasons to

---

78 Avery Dulles, A History of Christian Apologetics, 2nd ed. (Ignatius Press, 2005), xx.

hold to the general intellectual framework of the Christian faith and recognize the illumination and clarity it brings in contrast to other worldviews. Even if gray areas exist, we can still detect truth, beauty and goodness. But we should begin with what's clear and move to the unclear, rather than vice versa. As Samuel Johnson purportedly said, the existence of twilight isn't a good argument against the difference between day and night.[79] Consider what one former Muslim—eventually martyred for his Christian faith—discovered: "The more I study the world's religions, the more beautiful Jesus appears to me."

Fourth, we should reject the false and pernicious idea that knowledge requires 100 percent certainty. Virtually all epistemologists reject the notion that knowledge requires absolute certainty. Since the time of Descartes, who sought knowledge that is "self-evident, incorrigible, and evident to the senses," many in our culture assume, demand and crave this elusive standard.[80] They think that they can't have knowledge unless it's logically impossible they could be wrong. Unfortunately, many Christians have bought into this notion and routinely fall prey to perpetually second-guessing the Christian faith—"but what if...?"

---

[79] Mentioned in Alvin Plantinga, Warranted Christian Belief (New York: Oxford University Press, 2000), 202.

[80] René Descartes, Meditations and Selections from the Principles, trans. John Veitch (Chicago: Open Court, 1927).

As a result, they are immobilized by doubts and make no progress in their journey with God. Also, the absolutecertainty criterion can't sustain itself. How do we know with 100 percent certainty that knowledge requires 100 percent certainty? Paul writes, "For this you know with certainty..." (Eph 5:5); why add "with certainty" if knowledge *entails* certainty? It doesn't. Yet we can still have confident knowledge of God's love and acceptance—and excellent reasons for the Christian faith.

Fifth, those engaging in doubt should doubt fairly. This applies to atheists or agnostics demanding rigorous proofs for God's existence or the reality of objective moral values. Do they apply the same lofty standard to anything they themselves believe? Or are they operating by a double standard?

Consider the problem of evil. Skeptics may support their negative stance toward God by pointing to many baffling evils that appear pointless. So, they infer, God couldn't have a reason for them. But is this charge a fair one? Actually, no. For one thing, the skeptics aren't applying their skepticism symmetrically. Their standards for theism are likely much more stringent than their standards for theological unbelief or disbelief. Second, it doesn't follow that, just because a finite human like me doesn't know these reasons, an all-wise God couldn't have morally sufficient reasons for permitting these evils. We just aren't properly positioned to know the mind of God. It doesn't follow that inscrutable evils must be pointless. How do skeptics know with such great confidence that God, if he exists, could have no good reasons for permitting evil? Even if pointless evils do exist, some philosophers have reasoned that God still has a *general* purpose for such evils—to remind humans that all is not well in the world, to turn from their self-sufficiency and seek outside assistance from God (Lk 13:1-5).

Likewise, Christians who struggle with doubts about God's existence or Jesus' saving uniqueness shouldn't use a double standard themselves. They should consider *doubting their doubts.* It's a common assumption that if a belief can be doubted just a smidgeon, then we should always take those doubts seriously, succumb to them and remain in an epistemological no-man's-land. But this takes doubt much too seriously. After all, it's logically possible that the external world is illusory, that the universe isn't older than fifteen minutes and that other minds don't exist. But we never truly contest these things; we rightly take them as properly basic. So why do we trust our doubts more than we do our beliefs? Why think that doubting is somehow smarter than belief?

Notice too that even when we doubt, we are trusting the proper function of our rational capacities. This should prompt us to ask: "Where did these rational capacities come from? From nonrational, nonconscious, material processes? Why should I assume they're functioning properly?" Being made in the image of a rational, truthful God makes excellent sense of this fundamental trust we have that our cognitive faculties aren't systematically deceiving us and thus that we can seek after truth.

Sixth, we should sort out what kind of doubt we're facing. Is it intellectual, emotional, moral or spiritual? While many assume that all doubting is intellectual, very often it is not. When it is intellectual, the doubter should explore rational or evidential reasons for that doubt—as well as how the Christian faith addresses the deepest longings of our hearts. Many believers will experience times of doubt, but it is during the times of *stability* that we should explore the solid supports of our faith. We should take careful note of God's work through specific answers to prayer and clearly miraculous events we have witnessed or heard from trustworthy sources. We should enter such events into our journals and return to them in shakier times.

Yet here we must remember that mere "spectator evidence," as Paul Moser calls it, is inadequate because it remains disconnected from the human will. Many people know well the connection between smoking and lung cancer. But despite plenty of medical documentation and the Surgeon General's clear warning on cigarette packs, smokers continue in their habit. Likewise, why should God make himself obvious to the unwilling? Is God obligated to continually remind people of his presence much like a constant ringing in the ears or a perpetual throbbing headache? Some won't believe, Jesus said, even if someone comes back from the dead (Lk 16:31). Like a radio frequency available to all people, it is possible to tune out God's voice in creation or conscience by distractions, rationalization and suppression of the truth. We can have all the intellectual information we need about God's existence but still be unmoved in our spirit to obey.

Some doubt may be emotional. Emotional doubt tends to respond to even the most plausible answers with "Yes, but what if...?" Emotional doubts will never be satisfied with intellectual resolutions, no matter how solid and commonsensical they are. In this case, some people may be dealing with insecurities and anxieties—perhaps an experience with a negative or absent father-figure, which inclines them to doubt the heavenly Father—and such an issue may require counseling to move to greater self-insight and clarity about the problem. It's fascinating to note that the world's leading atheists or hard-nosed skeptics like Marx, Nietzsche, Freud, Sartre and Russell had one thing in common: they all had a negative to nonexistent relationship with the father-figure in their lives. Paul Vitz, who taught psychology at New York University, has documented this in his book *Faith of the Fatherless.* This point doesn't disprove atheism, but it reminds us that we are more than intellectual beings, and it challenges the notion that theists are somehow intellectually deficient and should be psychoanalyzed while atheists or skeptics are off the hook.

Moral doubt about God or objective moral values may spring from immoral inclinations or actions. As we've seen, the agnostic Aldous Huxley desired sexual freedom and easily constructed a philosophy to support it. We can come up with all sorts of intellectual-sounding rationalizations or doubts to evade objective moral truths and personal responsibility, or to keep a holy, unsafe God at a distance. For such persons, intellectual arguments for God's existence fall on deaf ears.

Spiritual doubt can be the result of struggles and discouragements with sin. Spiritual warfare may be a contributing factor to spiritual doubt. Satan is the accuser of believers, and Satan and his forces delight in reminding us of our sin and failure (Rev 12:10; Zech 3:1). Feeling that we're not good enough (and we aren't!) can incline us toward vainly striving to be accepted before God. Instead we should remind ourselves of the truth that acceptance before God has actually been accomplished by Christ on our behalf (Rom 15:7). In response, we should make it our ambition to be pleasing to God (2 Cor 5:9). This presupposes that God has already received us as his children. The Christian faith is a religion of gratitude. We can take further comfort from the fact that, the longer we walk with Christ, the more we realize how shot through with sin we are. Jonathan Edwards—a model of Christian dedication—wrote about feeling his profound sinfulness in terms of infinite upon infinite and infinite multiplied by infinite.[81] Yet detecting that "there is no health in us," as the Book of Common Prayer affirms, is actually an encouraging sign of spiritual health, and this awareness should prompt us to turn to God continually rather than wallow in despair.

Seventh, there is more to our identity than our feelings of doubt, and doubters can take steps to help strengthen or awaken faith. We live in an era that emphasizes being authentic—being true to our feelings, or finding ourselves. On the contrary, Jesus of Nazareth is the true human; so the way to truly find ourselves (Mt 16:25) is to become more like Jesus. It's possible to overemphasize our feelings. We aren't transformed by the renewing of our emotions or even of our circumstances, but of our minds (Rom 12:2). Paul wrote, "For I am conscious of nothing against myself, yet I am not by this acquitted; but the one who examines me is the Lord" (1 Cor 4:4). We are more than our fluctuating inner states. We possess a will that can resolutely trust in the character and promises of a faithful God—a will that also perseveres and endures when we feel like giving up. We have an intellect to grasp the rational and practical coherence of the Christian faith. We have a fellowship of believers who can share in our journey—its joys

---

[81] Jonathan Edwards, "Personal Narrative," in A Jonathan Edwards Reader, ed. John Smith, et al. (New Haven: Yale University Press, 2008), 294.

and sorrows, its glimmers of light and tunnels of darkness.

Some believers who want God to reveal himself may be looking in the wrong places. For one thing, if our experience becomes the full extent of our encounter with God, it will be shallow indeed. To more fully experience God's presence, we need to get out more! If Christ indwells our fellow believers, we can often glimpse God's presence through them as we read the Scriptures, pray, share in worship and the sacraments, and live life together with them. Our faith can be strengthened by the writings of the saints and their experiences of God. We can readily locate credible sources concerning the work of God through visions, healings and supernatural answers to prayer, which can encourage our faith. But unsettling feelings of doubt must not rule us. Instead we should take steps to put them in their proper place.

You may be familiar with the "Agnostic's Prayer," which goes something like this: "God, if there is a God, save my soul, if I have a soul." This sounds similar to the doubting father in the gospel story who cried out to Jesus, "I do believe; help my unbelief" (Mk 9:24). Others might say that they would *like* to believe in God, but they just find it difficult to do so. But here is an encouraging thought: such doubters can take certain concrete steps toward faith. In addition to considering the points above, they can undertake the "devotional experiment." The devotional experiment acknowledges that we cannot directly change our beliefs by simply wanting to, like flipping a switch; rather, we *assent* to certain things we find to be true. While some truths run counter to our feelings or our present frame of mind, we can exercise our will by *accepting* a belief to be true—by "reckoning" it so (Rom 6:11 KJV). For example, I can trust in God's promises in Christ over against my own doubts or the feelings of condemnation in my conscience (1 Jn 3:18-20).[82] And sometimes accepting those truths can lead to *assenting.* That is, we can choose to put ourselves into an environment that is conducive to producing—indirectly—a cluster of new beliefs.

> My whole heart strains to know what the true good is in order to pursue it: no price would be too high to pay for eternity.
>
> Blaise Pascal, *Pensées*

We can go farther. Rather than surrounding ourselves with cynics (Ps 1:1-2), we should diligently and patiently seek God where he is more likely to be found. Seekers and doubters can intentionally spend time with thoughtful, serious-minded, transformed believers and open themselves up to the experience

---

82 Paul J. Griffiths, Problems of Religious Diversity (Malden, MA: Blackwell, 2001), 26-30. Some of these thoughts are taken from Douglas V. Henry, "Does Reasonable Nonbelief Exist?" Faith and Philosophy 18/1 (January 2001): 75-92.

of the Christian community's love. They can meditate on Scripture, pray and read the stories of faithful Christians. While we can't choose our beliefs, we can choose our actions, through which we can better position ourselves to experience the reality of God and his influence in our lives.

Persistently unaddressed doubts can be immobilizing and even destructive to our faith. So we must, as poet John Donne urged, "doubt wisely."[83]

---

83 From Donne's poem "Satire III."

8

PURSUING PHILOSOPHY?

We've explored a number of themes in this book, and hopefully we've provided some grist for your mental mill as you consider the value, joys and challenges of philosophy. We've seen that philosophy need not be a dull, life-draining or irrelevant discipline. It can be a valuable ally as we face decisions or challenges, and not only in our spiritual lives. It is a fine and honorable discipline—and, for some, a calling—to pursue as a Christian. What are some indicators that can help you discern whether you should take this particular path? Here are a few considerations.

First, ask yourself, *Do I love philosophy?* Don't pursue fulltime philosophy if it doesn't deeply excite, enthrall and motivate you, even though it will mean hard, long and careful mental labor. Encountering towering philosophical minds—both past and present—should humble us and inspire a proper awe. Love for philosophy should be accompanied by intellectual modesty.

Another question to ask is, *Am I good at philosophy?* Of course, some are far more adept at philosophizing than others. Some may have to work much harder and longer than others. Those who make philosophy their life pursuit should at least be able to navigate through the rigors of a doctoral program—although studying philosophy at any level can be profitable and gratifying, as we've seen.

> I do not feel equal to the [philosophical] problems treated in this book. They seem to me to require an order of intelligence wholly different from mine. Others who have tried to address the central questions of philosophy will recognize the feeling.
>
> Thomas Nagel, *The View from Nowhere*

Third, ask yourself, *Could I spend my life doing this?* While you may be gifted in philosophy, you may have other gifts you would be wiser to focus on. Of course, philosophy can always serve as something of a handmaid to a different calling or pursuit that is even more suited to the way God has made you. Many have found that a solid undergraduate degree in philosophy is foundational for doing work in theology, law, politics or related fields. Training in philosophical reasoning brings with it a range of transferable skills.

If you do pursue philosophy, strive to become as well-rounded as possible. Work toward a good grasp of the basic branches of philosophy, even though you will likely specialize in one or two. Become familiar with philosophy's key figures and their chief ideas. Doing this is, of course, a tall order and a lifelong pursuit. Along with our philosophical work should come the quest for both deep biblical literacy as well as solid theological understanding, lest our philosophy become sub-biblical and a deviation from sound doctrine. Digesting Jaroslav Pelikan's five-volume series *The Christian Tradition* is a superb place to start.

Fourth, *Does philosophy enhance my pursuit of Christ-likeness?* Since our chief duties are to love God and to love others, we should ask whether philosophizing inhibits or facilitates this pursuit. Does the study of philosophy enhance and deepen my worship of God? Has my love for reading and studying the Word of God become a detached, academic exercise, or does it nourish me? Does philosophy lead me to become more disagreeable and contentious? Does it make me more insulated and antisocial? Do I withdraw from others who don't understand my philosophical jargon? Do I become more arrogant because those "plebians" around me haven't had the lofty and sophisticated training I've had? Does studying philosophy diminish my skill for living—that is, wisdom itself?

Of course, doing philosophy will require time alone to read, to study, to concentrate and to contemplate. Philosophy calls for solitude. Yet knowing this necessitates redoubling our efforts to pursue loving God and others. We must counteract the tendencies of self-absorption, pride and spiritual irrelevance. And as we've seen, much good philosophizing can be done in community. Indeed, our philosophical work can be nourished and enriched by our philosophical comrades-in-arms.

Ultimately, our philosophizing—as with our eating, drinking or whatever we do—should be done to the glory of God. Undertaking the study of philosophy should be an act of worship, and thus we devote our mental exertions, our research and our reading to God. Our philosophy should be undertaken in a spirit of prayer and dependence on God for understanding, insight and wisdom about what projects to undertake. The philosopher Martin Buber once said, "When one eats in holiness, when one tastes the flavor of the food in holiness, then the table becomes an altar."[84] Likewise, when we undertake philosophy in Christ's name, our desk or reading chair becomes an altar, yielding "a fragrant aroma, an acceptable sacrifice, well-pleasing to God" (Phil 4:18).

---

[84] Martin Buber, The Origins and Meaning of Hasidism. Cited in Donald J. Moore, Martin Buber: Prophet of Religious Secularism (Bronx, NY: Fordham University Press, 1996), 42. I have here used the more commonly-translated "holiness" instead of "consecration."

Finding the Textbook You Need

The IVP Academic Textbook Selector is an online tool for instantly finding the IVP books suitable for over 250 courses across 24 disciplines.

www.ivpress.com/academic/

Printed in Great Britain
by Amazon